Conceptual Change Model: The CCM Handbook

D1500773

DEDICATION

To the gentle and loving soul of

John William Schmidt

(April 3, 1978 – May 15, 2003)

Conceptual Change Model: The CCM Handbook

A constructivist model for designing, implementing, and assessing meaningful learning experiences that challenge student preconceptions and result in deep understanding

Diane L. Schmidt
Barbara Woodworth Saigo
Joseph I. Stepans

Foreword by Robert E. Yager

Saiwood Publications
© 2006
www.saiwood.com

Conceptual Change Model: The CCM Handbook
Diane L. Schmidt, Barbara Woodworth Saigo, Joseph I. Stepans

©2006, Saiwood Publications   Second printing January, 2007
ISBN10 0-9649967-5-8
ISBN13 978-0-9649967-5-5

For information about obtaining permission and for ordering copies of the book please contact:

Saiwood Publications
23051 County Road 75
St. Cloud, MN 56301 USA
www.saiwood.com
saiwood@aol.com
800-743-4787

Related titles. See at www.saiwood.com.

Teaching for K-12 Mathematical Understanding Using the Conceptual Change Model. (2005). Includes 112 CCM lessons.

Changing the Classroom from Within: Partnership, Collegiality, Constructivism, 2nd ed. (1999). Professional development using WyTRIAD.

Cover photograph: Energetic surf at Gleneden Beach, Oregon.
© B. W. Saigo, 2004

 Printing and binding by PALMER PRINTING, St. Cloud, Minnesota
Printed on recycled paper

FOREWORD

This wonderful new handbook provides assistance for teachers and future teachers who are familiar with the visions for teaching that are emphasized in the national standards. It offers ideas and procedures for change that make sense, using examples and situations common in the lives of all teachers.

This handbook has many strengths. The writing is clear, the context accurate, and the language user-friendly. Research is interpreted and its use encouraged. The ideas that are offered are tested and in keeping with the best recommendations for change, focusing not upon what to teach but on how to teach. The use of constructivist philosophy is commendable and appropriately presented.

Steps to student learning illustrate the model in down-to-earth ways, without jargon. The chapters include clear lists of what needs to be accomplished, desired student dispositions, teaching strategies, needed planning, problems that might arise, and ways of assessing success. These all speak to the reader and provide sign posts needed for accomplishing each phase. The suggestions for going further with the lessons are superb. Chapter 1 provides a great basis for the whole book.

One of the strengths of the handbook is the inclusion of four diverse lessons illustrating the model. They exemplify the advocacy that is central to the handbook and the examples give the reader more than dialogue, providing interpretations and explanations for each step of lesson development.

The handbook provides assistance for teachers and future teachers who are familiar with the visions for teaching that are emphasized in the *National Science Education Standards (NSES)*. The Conceptual Change Model utilizes all the recommendations of the *NSES* and the companion publication, *How People Learn*, to help teachers and encourage them to teach in ways that result in more and better learners. The handbook recognizes that how teachers teach is more important than what they teach.

If all new teachers and our best practicing teachers were to use the ideas in the handbook, it would add to our information base and accomplish more quickly what is currently happening in but one percent of the 3,000 school districts in the United States. Using these ideas would make our current efforts more universally accepted and we would save the several decades that it would take to change teaching for the majority of school age children in the United States.

Robert E. Yager

Science Education Center

The University of Iowa

May 2006

PREFACE

Purpose of this handbook

This handbook is a guide for designing and implementing lessons to bring about deep and meaningful understanding of the content that students are expected to learn. The Conceptual Change Model (CCM), developed by Dr. Joseph I. Stepans during the 1980s and early 1990s, is a formalization of the theoretical models arising from the research of Posner, Strike, Hewson, and Gertzog (1982), Strike and Posner (1985), and others.

It has proved successful for thousands of teachers who have used lessons published in previous Stepans books (1994, 2003, 2005) and who have created their own CCM lessons. It has been widely used in K-12 and college classrooms, including teaching methods courses.

The CCM is consistent with the best practices in teaching and learning highlighted in the National Science Teachers Association *Exemplary Science Program* monographs (NSTA, 2005a, 2005b, 2005c, 2006), the *National Science Education Standards* (NRC, 1996), and national standards in other curricular areas.

Constructivist philosophy and instruction

This small book concisely introduces the theory, research, and constructivist philosophy on which the six-phase Conceptual Change Model is based. In addition, this book will help the reader understand *why* each component of the model is important and provide guidance in *how* to develop and implement CCM lessons.

The CCM is based on the cumulative research on learning and teaching, particularly over the past three decades. Many references are cited, but they should be looked upon as only a sample of the relevant literature. Even a cursory review of the literature will reveal thousands of studies, articles, books, and commentaries about constructivist-based learning theory, teaching and assessment strategies, and classroom dynamics.

Related books

The CCM has been featured in books for science (Stepans, 1994; 2003), mathematics (Stepans, Schmidt, Welsh, Reins, Saigo, and Kansky [Ed.], 2005), and professional development (Stepans, Saigo, and Ebert, 1995, 1999). The science and mathematics books provide numerous classroom lessons. Readers unfamiliar with the CCM might want to try a lesson from one of these books (or this book) to get a feel for the process.

The third book features the CCM as the centerpiece of the Wyoming TRIAD (WyTRIAD), a nationally recognized professional development model, named in recognition of its state of origin. The WyTRIAD was one of 15 models nationwide identified by NSTA as an exemplary professional development process (NSTA, 2005a).

Some readers will be familiar with the previous books and may wonder how this book differs. Those books describe how to use the CCM in specific content areas. **This CCM handbook provides practical instruction on how to design, implement, and assess CCM learning experiences in any content area.** It relates new experiences to existing knowledge and skills. It also advises how to deal with reasons for failure or difficulties that may be encountered.

Intended audience

♦ This book is written for teachers, university educators, pre-service teachers, graduate students, professional development facilitators, home-schoolers, and anyone else interested in helping learners construct meaning from their educational experiences.

♦ It will be especially helpful to those who are already familiar with the CCM and who would like more information and support for using the model effectively.

♦ This book will be an excellent resource for methods courses, workshops, classroom teaching, and other situations that focus on inquiry-based lesson planning and teaching for understanding.

What's inside

The heart of the book is its attention to the view of learning as a process of conceptual change and the implications of that view for teaching. It explains how to develop CCM lessons that bring about deep understanding as learners gain insights into their own thinking and that of their classmates. It relates learning theory to practical applications.

Chapter 1 introduces the CCM and the historical and research basis of conceptual change approaches to learning and teaching.

Chapter 2 discusses factors to consider in preparing to design a CCM lesson, including identifying which topics, concepts, and skills should be addressed in the lesson.

Chapters 3-8 present guidance on developing and implementing the six phases of a CCM lesson. Each of these six chapters includes:

- An explanation of why the phase of the lesson is important to the learner and the learning process
- A description of what occurs in the phase
- A description of experiences the learner should have during that phase of the lesson
- A description of appropriate instructional strategies
- Guidance in planning that phase of the lesson
- Specific annotated examples of four lessons, illustrating how they were developed by the authors
- A description of the roles of the students and teacher during the implementation of that phase of the lesson
- Opportunities for assessing students' understanding and dispositions

Chapter 9 discusses the many opportunities for assessing the development of student understanding, skills, and dispositions. It provides concrete examples of appropriate assessment and sample rubrics. It also includes suggestions for evaluating the effectiveness of instruction.

References and **Appendices** conclude the book.

ACKNOWLEDGEMENTS

We wish to thank all of the teachers and pre-service teachers who have shared the challenges and difficulties they faced in creating their first Conceptual Change Model lesson.

A very special thank you to the incredible teachers in Jackson and Torrington, Wyoming, who took considerable time to provide the detailed comments included throughout the book.

We deeply appreciate the professional insights and contributions of our reviewers in guiding the final stages of manuscript development and for allowing us to share their comments. Brief professional summaries for our reviewers are located in Appendix IV.

Dr. Robert E. Yager, Professor of Science Education, Science Education Center, University of Iowa

Dr. James A. Shymansky, E. Desmond Lee Professor of Science Education at the University of Missouri-St. Louis

Dr. Diana Wiig, Department of Elementary and Early Childhood Education, University of Wyoming

Dr. Linda Ray, Professor of Literacy Education and Associate Dean of Undergraduate Studies, Florida Gulf Coast University

Mr. Timothy T. Couch, Jr., K-12 Professional Development Coordinator, Whitaker Center for Science, Mathematics, and Technology Education, Florida Gulf Coast University

TABLE OF CONTENTS

CHAPTER 1: THE CONCEPTUAL CHANGE MODEL 17
What is the Conceptual Change Model? 17
Profile of a Conceptual Change Model lesson 19
Looping or cycling back through CCM phases 20
Comparison to some other constructivist models 22
Comparison to traditional instructional models 22
Theoretical basis for the Conceptual Change Model 25
Powerful preconceptions 27
Supportive rationale and research 28
Misconceptions about the Conceptual Change Model 29
What have we learned from teachers? 30
Teachers' comments about the Conceptual Change Model ... 31

CHAPTER 2: WHAT DO WE WANT STUDENTS TO LEARN? 33
Difficulties and misconceptions associated with deciding what
    to teach 33
Effective methods for deciding what to teach 35
Conceptual understanding versus memorization 35
Identifying student conceptions 39
Recognizing where difficulties and misconceptions originate 41
Knowing what student learning looks like 42
In the next 6 chapters 43

CHAPTER 3: COMMIT TO A POSITION OR AN OUTCOME 45
What is the purpose of this phase? 45
What occurs in Commit to a Position or an Outcome? 46
Student dispositions we hope to see 46
What are some appropriate strategies? 47
How do we plan this phase of the lesson? 48
Detailed planning examples 50
How do we facilitate Commit to a Position or an Outcome? .. 52
What common problems occur in planning and facilitating this
    phase? 53
What do we assess during Commit to a Position or an
    Outcome? 54
Teachers' comments about Commit to a Position or an
    Outcome 55

CHAPTER 4: EXPOSE BELIEFS 57
What is the purpose of this phase? 57
What occurs in Expose Beliefs? 57
Student dispositions we hope to see 59
What are some appropriate strategies? 60

How do we plan this phase of the lesson? 60
Detailed planning examples... 61
How do we facilitate Expose Beliefs? 63
What common problems occur in planning and facilitating this
    phase?... 64
What do we assess during Expose Beliefs?........................ 64
Teachers' comments about Expose Beliefs....................... 65

CHAPTER 5: CONFRONT BELIEFS 67
What is the purpose of this phase? 67
What occurs in Confront Beliefs? 67
Student dispositions we hope to see 68
What are some appropriate strategies? 68
How do we plan this phase of the lesson? 71
Detailed planning examples... 72
How do we facilitate Confront Beliefs?............................ 75
What common problems occur in planning and facilitating this
    phase?... 77
What do we assess during this phase? 77
Teachers' comments about Confront Beliefs 78

CHAPTER 6: ACCOMMODATE THE CONCEPT 81
What is the purpose of this phase? 81
What occurs in Accommodate the Concept? 83
Student dispositions we hope to see 85
What are some appropriate strategies? 85
How do we plan this phase of the lesson? 86
Detailed planning examples... 87
How do we facilitate Accommodate the Concept?............. 89
What common problems occur in planning and facilitating this
    phase?... 90
What do we assess during Accommodate the Concept? 90
Teachers' comments on Accommodate the Concept.......... 91

CHAPTER 7: EXTEND THE CONCEPT 93
What is the purpose of this phase? 93
What occurs in Extend the Concept? 94
Student dispositions we hope to see 95
What are some appropriate strategies? 95
How do we plan this phase of the lesson? 96
Detailed planning examples... 96
How do we facilitate Extend the Concept? 98
What common problems occur in planning and facilitating this
    phase?... 99
What do we assess during Extend the Concept?................. 99
Teachers' comments about Extend the Concept..............100

CHAPTER 8: GO BEYOND 101
  What is the purpose of this phase? 101
  What occurs in Go Beyond? 101
  Student dispositions we hope to see 102
  What are some appropriate strategies? 103
  How do we plan this phase of the lesson? 103
  Detailed planning examples.......................................104
  How do we facilitate Go Beyond? 105
  What common problems occur in planning and facilitating this
      phase?..106
  What do we assess during Go Beyond?............................106
  Teachers' comments about Go Beyond...........................107

CHAPTER 9: ASSESSMENT AND THE CONCEPTUAL CHANGE MODEL
....109
  Assessment and evaluation.......................................109
  Pre-assessment..110
  Continuous assessment during a CCM lesson 114
  Assessing dispositions...115
  Assessing and grading content....................................117
  Student self-assessment 124
  Evaluation of instruction...124
  Assessment, evaluation, and continuous improvement 125

REFERENCES 127

APPENDIX I. COMPLETE SAMPLE CCM LESSONS 131
  Complete CCM lesson on Community Planning 131
  Complete CCM lesson on Density 132
  Complete CCM lesson on Word Recognition 133
  Complete CCM lesson on Understanding pi 134

APPENDIX II. CCM LESSON-PLANNING SUMMARY 135

APPENDIX III. ABOUT THE AUTHORS..................................137

APPENDIX IV. ABOUT THE REVIEWERS 140

APPENDIX V. A PROFESSIONAL INVITATION 143

APPENDIX VI. READER FEEDBACK REQUEST.........................144

OPENING THOUGHTS ABOUT PRECONCEPTIONS, ACHIEVING COMPETENCE, AND THE IMPORTANCE OF METACOGNITION [1]

Students come to the classroom with preconceptions about how the world works. If their initial understanding is not engaged, they may fail to grasp the new concepts and information, or they may learn them for purposes of a test but revert to their preconceptions outside the classroom.

To develop competence in an area of inquiry, students must (a) have a deep foundation of factual knowledge, (b) understand facts and ideas in the context of a conceptual framework, and (c) organize knowledge in ways that facilitate retrieval and application.

A metacognitive approach to instruction can help students learn to take control of their own learning by defining learning goals and monitoring their progress in achieving them.

From *How People Learn* (NRC, 2000)

---

[1] Metacognition refers to an individual's awareness of what he or she knows and how it is known. This self-understanding enables a person to make choices about what is needed to learn effectively (*e.g.*, nature of the learning environment, planning and scheduling, what strategies to use when learning and studying), understand and deal with reasons for failure or difficulty, and relate new experiences to existing knowledge and skills.

CHAPTER 1: THE CONCEPTUAL CHANGE MODEL

What is the Conceptual Change Model?

The Conceptual Change Model (CCM) is a six-phase process designed to bring about conceptual change in the learner. It was first designed as a method for teaching science and later applied to mathematics; however, teachers and professors have reported its applicability to all content areas. **Thus, this book serves as a guide for lesson development and implementation in any subject area.**

Because it is a learner-centered model, each phase is titled to describe the cognitive activity of the learner during that phase. The roles of the teacher and students in this model are quite different from those in traditional instructional models. In a CCM lesson, the teacher facilitates learning experiences rather than presenting and explaining information and procedures.

Effective use of the Conceptual Change Model also involves **meaningful assessments.** Pre-assessment of learners' ideas about targeted concepts and skills provides information necessary for setting meaningful expectations. It allows teachers to design instruction that meets the needs of their own students while aligning with curricular standards. The teacher uses ongoing and final assessments to determine how well the students meet the expectations.

The following CCM figure and lesson profile provide a description of the six phases of the model. Notice the emphasis on student cognition and metacognition in each phase.

The Conceptual Change Model (CCM)

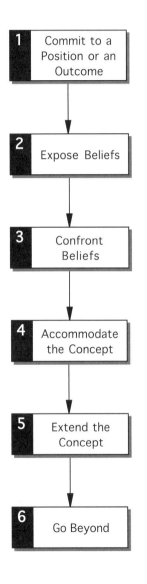

1 Commit to a Position or an Outcome	Students become aware of their own thinking by responding to a question or by attempting to solve a problem or challenge
2 Expose Beliefs	Students share and discuss their ideas, predictions, and reasoning with their classmates before they begin to test their ideas
3 Confront Beliefs	Students confront their existing ideas through collaborative experiences that challenge their preconceptions—working with materials, collecting data, consulting resources
4 Accommodate the Concept	Students accommodate a new view, concept, or skill by summarizing, discussing, debating, and incorporating new information
5 Extend the Concept	Students apply and make connections between the new concept or skill and other situations and ideas
6 Go Beyond	Students pose and pursue new questions, ideas, and problems of their own

Profile of a Conceptual Change Model lesson

The following section briefly describes the six phases of a CCM lesson in terms of what the learner experiences.

1. Commit to a Position or an Outcome

Before beginning a learning activity, students independently and privately acknowledge their current understanding through a thinking activity in which they write or illustrate their ideas in response to a question or challenge posed by the teacher. An important component of this phase is that students identify and record the reasons for their ideas. (See Chapter 3.)

2. Expose Beliefs

Next, each learner shares ideas with other group members. These small group discussions provide a safe venue for discussing ideas. As students listen to one another, they frequently find that others share beliefs similar to their own. Ideas from small groups are shared anonymously with the class as a whole. This sharing provides the opportunity for all students and the teacher to get a picture of the diverse perspectives represented in the class. (See Chapter 4.)

3. Confront Beliefs

After the *Expose Beliefs* phase of the lesson, learners are typically quite curious to find out if their thinking is correct. During the *Confront Beliefs* phase of the lesson, the learners engage in collaborative activities that enable them to test their ideas and to confront their current belief structures. These experiences require interpretation and may challenge existing views. (See Chapter 5.)

4. Accommodate the Concept

Through teacher-facilitated sharing and discussion of what the groups have learned, each learner comes to a new understanding that is based on the new experiences and consideration of the ideas presented by their peers and teacher. Each must find a way to accommodate this new information by reconciling it with existing ideas or restructuring current thinking. It is not expected that all learners will totally abandon their preconceptions and become convinced about the new ideas. (See Chapter 6.)

5. Extend the Concept

The lesson does not stop at that point. Students are encouraged to make connections between their new understanding and other real-life or academic experiences at home, at school, or elsewhere. They are given opportunities to share their ideas on where this concept is applied and to test out their new ideas or theories in a new context. (See Chapter 7.)

6. Go Beyond

This phase allows learners to come up with new questions of their own that help them think beyond the confines of the lesson. These new questions might be used for further class exploration, but they often lead to independent research and reading by the students. At this time, students have the opportunity to be creative as they consider completely new and intriguing ways to think about what they have learned. (See Chapter 8.)

Looping or cycling back through CCM phases

It is helpful to speak of the CCM as a sequence of phases, but that does not mean it is rigid. It actually flows seamlessly from phase to phase. There are even times when it is natural or desirable to loop back in the process before proceeding to *Extend the Concept* and *Go Beyond*, providing new challenges and experiences to reinforce concepts, deal with new or lingering misconceptions that have been revealed during the lesson, or introduce related concepts.

The following diagram illustrates some common points at which looping back logically occurs. It also indicates circumstances that are reasons for looping back.

Looping back within the CCM

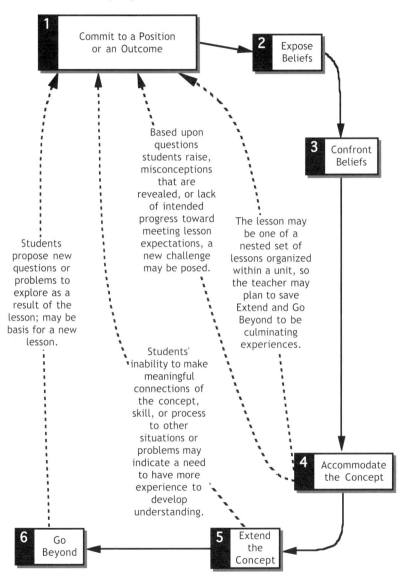

Comparison to some other constructivist models

Many readers may be familiar with other instructional models that align with constructivist theory but differ from the CCM.

♦ Most of them are three-step processes that are variations of the **Learning Cycle** (Atkins and Karplus, 1962; Karplus and Thier, 1967; Karplus and Lawson, 1974; Karplus, 1977; Erickson, 1979; Renner, 1982; Nussbaum and Novick, 1982; Renner and Marek, 1988; Lawson, 1988; Lawson, Abraham, and Renner, 1989).

♦ Several models define four or five stages (Barnes, 1976; Rowell and Dawson, 1983; Driver and Oldham, 1986; Boylan, 1988; Hewson and Hewson, 1988). Three of the best known four- or five-part models are the **Generative Learning Model** (GLM) (Osborne and Wittrock, 1983; Osborne and Freyberg, 1985; Osborne and Wittrock, 1985) the **BSCS 5-E Model** (Engage, Explore, Explain, Elaborate, Evaluate) (Bybee and Landes, 1990); and the **Constructivist Learning Model** (CLM) (Yager, 1993).

The CCM has many things in common with these models. It is distinctive, however, in the **extent** to which the teacher is a facilitator and to which student preconceptions are acknowledged, shared, challenged, discussed, and refined. A **unique feature** of the CCM is the sixth phase, in which the teacher encourages students to go beyond the lesson by asking them to pose new questions or ideas that they would like to explore.

Comparison to traditional instructional models

Most teachers have been taught to develop lessons following traditional models of instruction, such as the Madeline Hunter Model (Hunter, 2004). These traditional models call for a lesson sequence quite different from the CCM. The first notable difference is that the traditional model emphasizes what the **teacher** does, while the CCM focuses on the **learner**. A traditional lesson typically follows a sequence of about seven steps:

♦ Set the focus for the lesson
♦ Present learning objectives
♦ Review previous material
♦ Present new information and model skills

- ◆ Provide guided practice
- ◆ Provide independent practice
- ◆ Review or summarize learning

The first step of the traditional model is typically thought of as an attention-getter. On occasion, people talk about this as a step to activate the learner's prior knowledge. We need to ask ourselves, "What does it mean to activate prior knowledge?" For some, it means to remind students of what was taught in preceding lessons, while for others it implies asking students what they know. One commonly used strategy for this purpose is the KWL, a group process in which students brainstorm what they know and want to know about a topic before beginning the lesson.

Contrast this strategy to what occurs during the first two phases of a CCM lesson. Using the CCM, students first privately think about a problem or challenge, drawing upon their own understanding and personal, social, cultural, and academic experiences. They then share what they think with classmates and listen to what others have to say. These first two phases of a CCM lesson truly engage the learners and activate their prior knowledge.

Because everyone in the class participates in these phases of a CCM lesson, the students and the teacher become very aware of what everyone understands and recognize areas where there are uncertainties or confusion. Teachers frequently realize their assumptions about what students understand are quite different from what students actually bring to the classroom.

These beginning phases of a CCM lesson often reveal gaps in students' conceptual development. If these gaps are not identified and addressed, they widen, and eventually inhibit meaningful learning and contribute to negative attitudes and low self-esteem. On occasion, however, teachers may also discover that students have a more fully developed understanding than they expected. These CCM outcomes go well beyond attention getting.

Traditional instruction is premised on the belief that we should tell the students what we want them to learn at the start of the lesson and what steps will be taken in the process. This is not seen in the CCM or most other inquiry- or constructivist-based lessons. Constructivist educators begin lessons by challenging learners with interesting problems or dilemmas. The students quickly engage in figuring out what they need to learn in order to meet the challenge.

We often find that what students need to learn is different from what we think they need to learn.

In the CCM, there is no need to spend time reminding students of what we covered in previous lessons. The challenge we pose in the opening phase of the lesson will engage students in drawing on or connecting to their previous learning and personal experiences related to the new content.

The fourth stage of traditional instruction involves the teacher in the process of carefully presenting and explaining new information to students. This is probably the most difficult habit to break for teachers learning to use the CCM. In a CCM lesson, there is rarely a need for the teacher to formally present information or explain things to students. Rather, a CCM lesson requires the teacher to act as a facilitator, posing questions and providing resources for student exploration and research. Students go through an active process of making sense of things. During this process, they may borrow or incorporate ideas from their observations, classmates, and resources.

Ultimately, the learners explain their understanding of the concepts in a CCM lesson, and the teacher poses questions that will cause students to reconsider flawed or incomplete thinking. By the end of a CCM lesson, students generally have a much stronger understanding than that with which they started. The beauty of the CCM is that both the students and teacher are very aware of the depth of understanding gained.

The traditional instructional approach allows time for carefully taught and monitored skill practice. By contrast, the CCM and other inquiry models provide time for the learners to make, discover, and correct errors. Learners in a CCM lesson are asked to find their errors and explain them. Traditional practice involves the teacher in catching student errors and explaining those errors to the students. In the case of traditional independent practice, the teacher might simply grade the work or painstakingly write comments and make corrections that go unread, unnoticed, or are given only superficial attention by the learner. The CCM recognizes the importance of the learner in learning.

At the close of a traditional lesson, the teacher summarizes what was presented and frequently reviews

> We simply cannot think for students, but must expect and inspire them to think for themselves.

the common errors that were recognized during practice periods. As noted earlier, CCM lessons are very different, in that students are asked to use their own words to explain their learning to one another and to the teacher. However, this process goes further, in that students are also asked to make connections to other personal experiences and knowledge. They are then given an opportunity to ask their own questions and pose their own problems. These last three phases of the CCM provide great insight for the teacher in planning future learning experiences for students.

Project 2061 (Rutherford and Ahlgren, 1990; AAAS, 1993) and various national content standards emphasize that shallow exposure or "coverage" of a broad range of topics does not develop depth of understanding. In mathematics, for instance, students commonly learn algorithms or procedures to solve computational problems without understanding the underlying mathematical principles. In history classes, students may memorize names, dates, conflicts, and treaties, with no ability to connect what was going on at that time in intellectual thinking, the arts, and conditions of living, let alone simultaneous events in various parts of the world. For example, the War Between the States in the United States happened at about the same time as the Meiji Restoration in Japan, although most people probably think the end of the Samurai era occurred much earlier.

Sadly, in some ways the limited understanding and proficiency in a content area that results from instruction that does not acknowledge, respect, and adequately challenge the prior conceptions of a learner is similar to what happens to a large moth that emerges from its cocoon confined in a small jar. The wings are there, but they cannot expand and become functional. They are permanently deformed. The key to successful teaching for conceptual change is listening to what students say about what they think and their explanations for those beliefs, and then providing opportunities to liberate and expand their understanding, curiosity, and confidence.

Theoretical basis for the Conceptual Change Model

Making decisions about how we teach should be based on current theory and research by experts in the field. As with students, teachers and administrators must be convinced of the value of a new strategy.

The Conceptual Change Model is grounded in the **constructivist** paradigm of learning, which holds that knowledge is personally constructed as a result of an individual's experiences. This philosophy is supported by many renowned educational theorists, including Dewey, Piaget, and Vygotsky. According to constructivist theorists, learning occurs as the brain attempts to make sense of what it perceives, integrating new information into a matrix of existing knowledge and understanding. Even information that is presented directly, as through a lecture or textbook, passes through the filter of prior experiences and understanding.

Learners may enter the educational setting without preconceptions about a topic or concept, with naïve or flawed conceptions, or with misconceptions. The traditional learning environment may or may not assist them and their teachers in recognizing and altering their conceptions. This book is devoted to helping educators plan instruction that accounts for what students bring to the classroom and how they learn.

The works of many theorists, cognitive psychologists, and researchers have contributed to our current constructivist-based theory of learning and philosophy of teaching. The influence of several of them, in particular, can be recognized in the CCM.

♦ John Dewey emphasized the essential connection between direct experiences and learning, emphasizing that field, civic, service, and work experiences, and classroom simulations provide real-world and meaningful contexts for learning (Dewey, 1938).

♦ Jean Piaget may be the most often-cited contributor to present constructivist philosophy. His emphasis on learning through discovery incorporated the idea that a new experience challenges an existing mental framework or schema, creating a tension or disequilibrium that the mind then struggles to relieve by restructuring the existing schema to accommodate the experience or information (Piaget, 1964, 1969).

♦ Lev Vygotsky emphasized that learning is both a social and an individual process. His influence is a foundation for our current emphasis on having students collaborate as they work out their ideas (Vygotsky, 1978).

♦ Reuven Feuerstein is best known for his work on mediated learning experiences, recognizing that teachers have a critical role to play, not only in providing lessons, but also in guiding students to become metacognitive—to actively question and think about their own learning (Feuerstein, 1980).

♦ Howard Gardner proposed a theory of multiple intelligences, liberating teachers and learners from a narrow view of intelligence, preferred modes of learning, and assessment of academic performance (Gardner, 1983).

♦ The work of these theorists has been supported and informed by our increased understanding of neurophysiology, including research on how the brain functions to process sensory impulses and create memories. This work has demonstrated that there is a physical mechanism for learning. A pioneer in this work has been Marian Diamond (Diamond and Hopson, 1998).

Much writing has been devoted to describing and debating various points of constructivist philosophy and the nature of mental frameworks (Glynn and Duit, 1995; Duit and Treagust, 1998). Bell (1993) succinctly summarizes a view of learning as conceptual change, citing the importance of instruction that allows students to experience cognitive dissonance. She emphasizes that learning involves both constructing new conceptions and restructuring old ones.

Powerful preconceptions

It cannot be assumed that desired understanding results from exposure to good explanations of the content, strong—even charismatic—teaching, or entertaining lessons. Preconceptions are inventions of the mind of each individual in response to personal experiences. As a result, an individual is likely to be very comfortable with them.

Teaching for conceptual change requires acknowledging that pre-existing conceptions must be identified by both learner and teacher. Ausubel (1963, 1968) noted that prior knowledge can be extremely tenacious and difficult for learners to give up. Therefore, instructional experiences should be deliberately designed to challenge these preconceptions.

Posner, Strike, Hewson, and Gertzog (1982) and Strike and Posner (1985) suggest that genuine learning, or conceptual change, requires the following conditions:

♦ Students must be dissatisfied with their existing views.

♦ The new conception must appear somewhat plausible.

♦ The new conception must be more attractive.

♦ The new conception must have explanatory and predictive power.

If these four conditions are met, a learner is likely to successfully modify existing beliefs about a concept. Notice that the emphasis is on what happens **within** the learner. Simple **exposure** to new information or a new view is not enough to invoke conceptual change. Students may memorize facts and definitions and be able to reproduce them, but may not be able to make appropriate and useful connections among ideas that will allow for applications to real-world situations or problems that are more advanced.

The Conceptual Change Model addresses all of the above conditions, beginning with students becoming aware of their own thinking. Through a series of developmental phases, it helps them confront their views, refine them if necessary, and then immediately explain and use their new understandings.

Supportive rationale and research

The research-based rationale for each phase of the CCM is also reflected in *How People Learn* (Bransford, Brown, and Cocking, 2000). In the Executive Summary sections on "Transfer of Learning" and "Children as Learners," the authors synthesize key research findings, including:

♦ Skills and knowledge should be able to extend beyond the original learning context.

♦ Learners should be able to recognize when it is appropriate to apply what has been learned.

♦ Rote-memory learning is rarely transferable; instead, "transfer most likely occurs when the learner knows and understands underlying principles that can be applied to problems in new contexts."

♦ Conceptual knowledge assists independent learning.

♦ Metacognition is important to learning success. The learner who is self-aware and self-appraising is likely to become an independent, self-sustaining, life-long learner.

♦ Children are able to reason, even if they have limited knowledge and experience, and even though their logical abilities are not yet fully developed.

♦ Combined with their eagerness to learn, children's immature mental processes can lead to misunderstanding and development of misconceptions. (See box.)

♦ It is important to help children develop intentional learning strategies.

> "Precocious knowledge may jump-start the learning process, but because of limited experience and undeveloped systems for logical thinking, children's knowledge contains misconceptions. Misinformation can impede school learning, so teachers need to be aware of the ways in which children's background knowledge influences what they understand. Such awareness on the part of teachers will help them anticipate children's confusion and recognize why the children have difficulties grasping new ideas." From Executive Summary, *How People Learn (NRC, 2000)*

♦ "Children are both problem solvers and problem generators." They like to try to solve problems, seek new challenges, and learn from prior successes and failures. They are persistent and motivated by "success and understanding."

♦ Adults play an important role, helping children "make connections between new situations and familiar ones." Adults support and guide learning, playing off the natural curiosity and persistence of children, while paying attention to appropriate levels of difficulty and complexity.

Misconceptions about the Conceptual Change Model

Over the years, the following misconceptions about the CCM have been expressed by educators. We hope that these ideas will be adequately addressed in the following chapters.

♦ It is just the traditional scientific method.
♦ It is the well-known KWL.
♦ It is the same as the 1960's Learning Cycle.

We have heard teachers resist using the CCM, with statements revealing trepidations about veering from traditional instruction.

♦ It will take too much time.

♦ I will not be able to cover everything that my students are expected to learn.

♦ This will never work with my students.

♦ My students will not participate.

♦ My students will get too wild.

♦ Students would get bored if we did this every day.

♦ It will not work with large classes.

♦ I cannot get through all the phases of a CCM lesson in a single period.

♦ The CCM is not appropriate for all curricular areas.

What have we learned from teachers?

Teachers who are experienced in the use of the CCM have countered all the concerns expressed above. In reality, the use of the CCM does not necessarily require more time than traditional models. In fact, the depth of understanding developed by learners usually decreases the time typically needed for review and continuous re-teaching of content.

Students enjoy the opportunity to interact, and contrary to concerns by many teachers, the level of interaction increases in classrooms employing the CCM. Students who are traditionally quiet in class or those who are often considered to be weak students tend to thrive. The opportunity to draw upon their own personal experiences enables all students to safely contribute to the class discussions.

The structure of class lessons may seem to be repetitious, but the variety of strategies that can be employed in a CCM lesson is endless. Because of the increased interactions, neither students nor teachers experience boredom with the model. In fact, teachers frequently become absorbed in listening to the ways students express their understanding and the connections they make to other experiences and phenomena.

Teachers are often surprised to find that students who do not typically perform well in traditional classrooms take to the CCM format quickly. These students have the opportunity to recognize that they understand many things that are valuable to the learning process, and they have the opportunity to share this with others. We take immense joy in seeing students who may be considered as under-performing or poorly performing in traditional classrooms emerge as stars during the CCM lessons. Watching these students demonstrate strong learning and gain stature and respect from their peers is probably the most reward any teacher could hope to receive.

Teachers' comments about the Conceptual Change Model

♦ "I like how CCM promotes thinking and collaboration. I also feel CCM helps students gain a greater understanding of concepts. It helps you see your students in a different way. The teacher needs to let students take charge of learning."

♦ "The model allows students to commit to an idea on paper and then share it with their peers. I know they learn so much from one another. They pick up on new vocabulary and it allows them to share their ideas in a safe environment. I also like how it has students confront any misconceptions they may have on a particular concept."

♦ "The model requires and encourages real thinking. I am afraid children today have so much done for them that they don't even think for themselves. This method pushes them—they can't weasel out!"

♦ "The major strengths would be how engaged the students are, how deep their thinking goes, how much I learn about their knowledge by letting them talk and explore. The experience seems to stick with them longer."

♦ "These are rich experiences and teach kids things they will never forget."

♦ "It creates meaningful learning for the students. It helps to involve all abilities and learning styles."

♦ "CCM engages all students to be actively involved in their learning. It promotes learning among different learning styles. It varies instruction... individual, small group, whole group. It can change or clarify misconceptions."

♦ "My favorite part of CCM is where the children experiment to prove their predictions. They are able to discover their answers on their own. I like when they work with their peers. I like to listen to their conversations about math and whatever. They like math and want to learn."

♦ "Students work together and are engaged. There is increased willingness to take risks. They gain better concrete understanding of concepts through hands-on activities with students actively involved. These are more interesting (minds-on) and fun for students and teacher. The teacher acts as a facilitator of learning."

In the words of a teacher, "The beauty of the Conceptual Change Model is that it provides the purest structure for meeting the needs of diverse learners. The development of the intended concepts is not limited by age or ability. All students have the opportunity to grow from wherever they are when they begin the lesson. The model recognizes, values, and accepts everyone's experiences and perspectives. No matter what the students' levels of understanding at the beginning of the lesson, they all grow and explain their understanding throughout."

CHAPTER 2: WHAT DO WE WANT STUDENTS TO LEARN?

Difficulties and misconceptions associated with deciding what to teach

Textbook-driven planning

Most experienced teachers understand that what we teach should be determined largely by national and state standards, local curriculum guides, and approved course outcomes. However, common practice among teachers at all levels is to follow the textbooks that are adopted. This often results from teachers' own lack of confidence in themselves as instructional experts. In addition, limited time for planning and the belief that textbooks were carefully selected to meet the standards and curriculum outcomes provide further rationale for relying on textbooks to guide instruction.

We run into a number of problems when we make these assumptions about textbooks, however. First, textbook adoption committees usually rely on publisher claims of alignment to standards. Publishers frequently provide correlation documents that show how all national, and in some instances, state standards are addressed in their textbooks. What most educators do not realize is how these correlations are made. In some instances these correlations are done by word searches, in which key words from the standards are searched for in the text. When a match is made, that section of the text is marked as correlated to the standard. In other instances, more careful correlations are done. Even in these correlations, standards may be matched to text sections that provide ever-so-slight relationships to the standards.

To further illustrate how this could be possible, consider this. In 1996, when the *National Science Education Standards* (NRC, 1996) were first released, a national meeting was held inviting representatives from every major publisher. Only one showed up. When asked why, the publisher present said it was too risky for publishers to base their texts on standards, as it's not what teachers buy—they buy based on what is on the state and district tests.

During a curriculum-mapping activity with high school teachers, we asked teachers to randomly select a standard from their correlation guide and look up the sections of the textbook that covered the standard. After several trials, the teachers discovered that many of the standards they selected were not adequately covered in the text. In fact, some of the standards they selected were not even remotely addressed by the text. For example, one state standard related to assessing environmental impacts of human decisions. The section of the text to which the publisher correlated this standard was devoted to the periodic table. After very careful scrutiny by the teachers, they found the word "environmental" in the text, but it referred to where an element was found naturally in the environment. In addition to finding numerous instances of superficial or no coverage of the standards, these teachers also discovered that a large section of the textbook, which was very difficult for students and took them weeks to teach, was not mentioned in the state or national standards. As you can probably guess, they decided to quit covering that section of the textbook.

In another instance, teachers were working on vertically aligning curricular activities and assessments as a K-12 district initiative. High school teachers were quite surprised that they were teaching the same concept with the same expectations as fourth-grade teachers. This is frequently true about what is being tested.

Even when textbooks are selected carefully because of their coverage of course outcomes and sequence, we need to remember that textbooks often lag behind in currency of content, research, national expertise in the field, and current teaching practices. Additionally, recent advances in content knowledge are sometimes plugged into texts without consideration of developmental appropriateness or conceptual connections.

There is seldom a perfect fit between textbooks and the learning environment. It is important for us, as educators, to understand that we are responsible for designing daily instruction and selecting the resources that foster student understanding of the essential skills and concepts. It is never appropriate to plan instruction based solely on the textbook, but segments of the textbook can and should be used effectively to support teacher-designed instruction.

Textbooks are resources with long lists of topics and activities, but they are not the curriculum. We must remind ourselves that we are the experts responsible for meeting our students' learning needs. Therefore, we must be disciplined and knowledgeable about how best to choose and use textbooks and other learning resources with our students.

Selecting topics of interest to students

Understanding the importance of interest and motivation to student learning, we frequently select topics for instruction because they are of special interest to us or to our students. A favored topic can be very effective, if we use the topic as a means of focusing on the standards and course outcomes. This is probably more often true in K-8 classrooms. However, we often select the topic and then immediately, and quite naturally, begin thinking of motivational activities related to the topic. Too often, we find that these fun activities were very engaging for students, but on careful examination, they really did not help the students develop an understanding of the intended focus of the standard or objective. They may be interesting and entertaining, but ultimately irrelevant and ineffective.

Effective methods for deciding what to teach

Good planning begins with knowing what we want students to learn and be able to do, and this comes from examining standards, curriculum guides, and course goals and objectives for the level of our students. Once we have a clear understanding of what students are supposed to know and be able to do, it is fine to think about topics that would interest students, but we should refrain from planning activities until we think about specific learning expectations or objectives.

We might ask ourselves such questions as:

♦ What misconceptions or difficulties might students have?

♦ Where do the misconceptions or difficulties originate?

♦ Is the content focus something that requires more than memorization of facts and procedures?

♦ If the content focus is memorization of facts or procedures that are important for future applications, what are the associated concepts that will aid in understanding and memorization?

♦ What will student understanding look like?

Conceptual understanding versus memorization

Focusing on concepts related to the content will contribute to the design of activities that will help students:

- Develop a deep understanding of the content
- Be cognizant of their levels of understanding
- Increase their ability to apply their understandings in new situations
- Increase their capacities for retaining information
- Develop real interest in the subject matter
- Generate new questions that intrigue them and motivate them for further study and learning

Examining and analyzing curricular standards and benchmarks helps us focus on important concepts. The goal is to determine what the curriculum developers consider most important. This is not always easy to discern, and the difficulty can be confounded by the way standards are developed. Most K-12 national and state standards are written with benchmarks for grade bands (typically K-2, 3-5, 6-8, 9-12) rather than specific grade levels. District curriculum guides may help in specifying grade-level expectations. Nevertheless, it is important for the teacher to understand this progression and how the specific grade-level expectations relate to the broader benchmark and standard. Postsecondary courses often have a combination of very broad outcomes and a highly focused list of topics to be covered. Faculty members decide what major concepts are critical to understanding the discipline for the level of the course and how to present them.

Curriculum is typically developed in a hierarchical fashion, frequently based on the expert-defined structure of the content and its applications. Developing a concept chart or diagram can greatly assist in understanding how more specific concepts are successively grouped into more general categories. The following discussion is a very simplistic view of how concepts can be sorted.

In the tree diagram that follows, each concept is a noun that refers to a category of specific things. Knowing **how** categories are derived can help learners develop basic and broad understanding of the content. By contrast, merely memorizing the categories can preempt deeper conceptual understanding, limiting our abilities to generalize and apply information. For example, we might ask ourselves how we distinguish a table from a desk. We are very capable of making this distinction when we see them, but we may not be consciously aware of the criteria we use to distinguish these two categories of furniture. To become cognizant we need to spend some time thinking about both form and function of these objects.

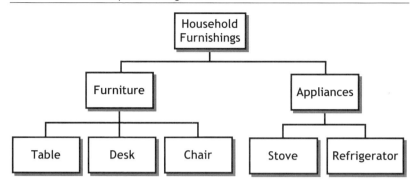

From this little exercise, you may notice that you have applied an understanding of furniture concepts at an unconscious level. So, why do we need to understand categories at a conscious level? Simply memorizing all of the items that are considered tables and all of the items that are considered desks does not create understanding that enables us to classify new objects.

Learning involves recognizing patterns and relationships that allow us to categorize. Successful learners are continually engaged in these processes. Too often, we enter learning environments where we are asked to memorize facts and procedures and our attention is drawn away from understanding the system in which they exist.

Curricula and textbooks rely on a hierarchical structure of content to sequence learning and develop textbooks. This is nearly always done in a very linear manner moving from the simplest or most fundamental concepts at the bottom of the hierarchy to the complex concepts at the top; for example, from atoms to molecules to cells to organisms to the environment.

The assumption is that in order to understand something in the middle of a hierarchy, learners must understand those things below it. This is a very logical sequence for those who are experts in the content and reflects how content is traditionally taught, rather than how most of us learn. There are inherent problems with this assumption and practice. First, even the most novice learners have prior experiences with concepts on various levels of the hierarchy. Second, students may have a problem with relevance—I do not need to understand how my car works in order to operate and maintain it effectively. It might help, but it is not necessary.

A third problem with this logic involves the disconnection the learner experiences. Memorizing discrete facts and information without understanding why or how they are connected to the rest of the discipline is very difficult for and boring to many students. This is what prompts the question most educators dread, "Why do we have to learn this?" We often do not have a good answer to this question, as we might not be sure why we are teaching that particular skill or concept. A teacher's understanding of the content domain can be extraordinarily important in helping learners develop understanding if used to guide exploration and accommodation, but not if used as a mechanism for linear sequencing of instruction.

While it **is** often very important for students to have an understanding of pre-requisite skills and concepts, this does not imply and necessitate linear teaching. By posing interesting and challenging questions and dilemmas, we give students opportunities to figure out or recognize what they need to learn in order to effectively answer the question or meet the challenge. Presenting a challenge from a step higher in the hierarchy can provide the motivation, connections, and interest students need to learn those basic skills and concepts.

When we think about what we want students to learn, we need to think about the system in which the content exists. For example, we may think of multiplication facts as something that must simply be memorized. Taking a conceptual or systems view of multiplication facts, however, might cause us to reconsider this notion. When students use only memorization to learn multiplication, they view each fact as discrete. This task might be likened to trying to memorize 100 definitions for unfamiliar terms in unfamiliar content areas without any phonemic cues such as familiar prefixes or suffixes.

Rather than starting with memorization of facts, students should first have opportunities to develop a strong concept of multiplication. Once the concept is understood, they should be able to apply it by showing 4 x 8 as four groups of eight and creating word problems that represent the fact. Although students must ultimately memorize facts, we can provide challenges that will motivate and help them in this process. For example, we might ask children to explain how 4 x 8 is related to 4 x 7 or 4 x 4. As they think about 4 x 8 being 4 more than 4 x 7 or twice as much as 4 x 4, they are developing an understanding of the system, flexibility in their thinking, strategies for memorizing, and strategies for recall if they forget a fact.

We might assume that students will recognize patterns and relationships as they begin memorizing, but that is not always true. We need to plan activities that will draw their attention to the patterns and relationships. For example, rather than focusing our instruction on "memorizing the 4 facts," we might do better to develop expectations that focus on the learner "developing strategies to memorize the 4 facts" or "recognizing the relationship of the 4 facts to the 2 facts."

Spelling and phonics are two other areas where pattern recognition is crucial for early learners. Traditional instruction is often designed with this in mind, but the learners may go through the activities without ever recognizing those patterns. For example, traditional spelling books group words by pattern, but if students are not asked to discover or explain the pattern they may never notice it or develop a conscious level of recognition. The same may be true for advanced high school and college level content. Animal and plant taxonomies, for instance, are more easily memorized if the system is first understood. More importantly, understanding enables students to use the system to identify relationships and classify specimens. Beginning instruction with a challenge, such as classifying an unknown plant, provides reason and motivation for students to develop that understanding.

Effective learning requires that students be mentally active in the pattern recognition and classification processes that are fundamental to conceptual understanding, memorization, and applications. Providing contextual, problem-solving challenges from the content, real life, and across content areas demonstrates the relevance and need for understanding the content and developing the skill.

Identifying student conceptions

As we think about specific lesson expectations, it helps to look beyond the standards and curriculum. Understanding the common misconceptions and areas of confusion related to the content is extraordinarily helpful. There are good and not-so-good methods for uncovering these. (See Chapter 9 for an expanded discussion of pre-assessing student understanding.) Some effective procedures involve:

- ◆ Thinking about our own experiences
- ◆ Analyzing previous student work
- ◆ Paying attention to questions students ask
- ◆ Listening to students' discussions about a topic
- ◆ Reading what experts say
- ◆ Conducting student interviews

Most of us have had the experience of planning a lesson and recognizing there was something we, ourselves, did not quite understand. Many of us have also discovered that we had misconceptions about certain phenomena as we researched what we were planning to teach. We often realize that we had these misconceptions as youngsters and never had the opportunity to confront them. Furthermore, most of us still hold misconceptions and naïve ideas of which we are yet unaware.

A second strategy for uncovering misconceptions is to examine students' actual work samples. Since it is very possible for students to pass tests without developing the desired understanding, we need to look beyond right and wrong answers and focus on how students explained a concept or how they completed a process. For example, looking at how a student completed a ratio problem may shed some light on the student's understanding of ratios. Alternatively, examining a student's concept map may reveal a great deal about the complexity of the student's understanding of the concepts represented.

Classroom observations can be very useful in identifying what students are thinking about concepts. The questions they ask reveal a great deal about their understanding, areas and sources of confusion, and misconceptions to which they may be clinging. Listening to students as they discuss their ideas in small groups can also shed light on their views, the connections they are making to personal experiences, the logical or illogical paths of thinking they are following, and possible difficulties they encounter as they try to explain their ideas.

Many experts have conducted research on students' ideas, explanations, and misconceptions, especially regarding natural phenomena. Reading the results of this research can be shocking to many teachers, but has great value. Knowing the common difficulties and understanding how they are formed can help us design instruction that will assist students in recognizing and changing their naïve or non-expert versions—or better yet—prevent misconceptions from developing.

Finally, the most effective way to uncover what students understand or misunderstand related to concepts we plan to teach is to interview several students individually. Effective interviews first use open-ended questions that ask students to explain their understanding. These prepared questions are followed by probing questions that ask for further explanation. Probing questions are frequently "why" and "how" questions that get the interviewees to stop and think deeply to determine the mental constructs they are using to justify their beliefs. (See also Chapter 9.)

Recognizing where difficulties and misconceptions originate

Student misconceptions can be attributed to the way in which learners process new information in relation to existing ideas. Difficulties can be compounded by instruction and inappropriate instructional materials. Knowing how instruction can lead students astray can help us determine appropriate learning objectives. Misconceptions can be attributed to such things as:

- ♦ Textbooks that contain errors, simplistic explanations, and overemphasis on definitions
- ♦ Non-realistic diagrams and physical models
- ♦ Two-dimensional representations of three-dimensional phenomena
- ♦ Teachers' misunderstandings they inadvertently share with students
- ♦ Students' lack of conscious awareness of their own beliefs
- ♦ Inability of learners to connect their own experiences to the content as presented
- ♦ Insufficient time devoted to students' questions

Some of this confusion can be avoided by focusing instruction on higher-order skills that require students to make connections and synthesize their learning. Asking students to justify their conclusions or evaluate the results of their study will lead them to recognize discrepancies between what they experience during the lesson and their initial beliefs and understandings.

To minimize our role in the development of misconceptions and confusion, it may be helpful to test and refresh our own understanding of the content. We might begin by developing our own concept map of what we plan to teach (Novak and Cañas, 2006). This involves mapping out the hierarchical arrangement of concepts using lines and connecting phrases to define the relationships between concepts. (See Chapter 9.) As we create these maps and discuss them with colleagues, we are likely to recognize gaps in our own thinking, as well as some mistaken ideas. Using a variety of resources, we can increase our own understanding of the concepts **before** we begin designing instruction.

Knowing what student learning looks like

Once we know what students should learn and be able to do and the misconceptions they bring to the learning environment, we can define what understanding will look like. This point takes us back to the notion of writing lesson expectations or objectives. Most teachers are taught to write these, but abandon the practice once in the classroom. However, there is great value to **describing how you will recognize understanding**. From reading the previous sections it may be evident that focusing on concepts and higher-level cognition will assist in designing learner expectations and lesson plans that help students to gain deeper understanding.

Still, we need to decide if we want to focus on a very broad topic or macro-concept that requires understanding of multiple concepts and processes or if we want to focus more narrowly on a somewhat isolated concept or process. There isn't a right or wrong decision here; however, we need to recognize that an expectation based on a broad topic or concept may require significantly more time to develop. In fact, these broad expectations might be thought of as unit goals or outcomes.

As we finalize our decision about the focus of our lessons, it is important to remember that our instructional goals include attention to students':

- ♦ Conceptual understandings of knowledge and skills
- ♦ Applications and connections
- ♦ Ability and willingness to experience a conceptual change
- ♦ Dispositions and habits of mind

In the next 6 chapters

Each of the following six chapters is devoted to one phase of the CCM. Each chapter provides the rationale and purpose of the phase, a description of what occurs during the phase, appropriate instructional strategies, guidance in planning and facilitating the lesson, the roles of the students and the teacher, and assessment opportunities. Also in Chapters 3-8, the authors explain their thinking in the development of sample lessons in social studies, science, language arts, and mathematics. The four complete lessons, as used with students, are located in Appendix I.

CHAPTER 3: COMMIT TO A POSITION OR AN OUTCOME

What is the purpose of this phase?

Teachers frequently ask, "How do I get my students to be more involved in class?" or "How can I motivate my students?" Many teachers attempt to involve and motivate students with hands-on activities. Although students may enjoy hands-on experiences, we need to ask ourselves whether these actually contribute to students' conceptual understanding and skill development. It is our belief that there should be a carefully considered reason for doing a hands-on activity. Hands-on may or may not be the best way to foster learning; however, "minds-on" is always desirable, because thinking is a necessary component of meaningful learning (Bonwell and Eison, 1991).

To create an effective learning environment, we ask, "What do I want to accomplish? What is the best way to proceed?" **The CCM involves and motivates students by focusing their energies on what we want them to gain from the learning experience.** The first phase of a CCM lesson engages the learner in thinking deeply about a challenge posed by the teacher. The teacher figuratively "grabs" the learners' minds to involve and motivate them intellectually.

Much of our educational system involves giving answers to questions our students never ask. Often, teachers focus students' attention on the content by beginning a topic in the following ways:

♦ Showing a video

♦ Outlining the objectives to be achieved

♦ Using an attention-getting demonstration

♦ Giving an historical account of the content

♦ Drawing a diagram and explaining its relevance or content

♦ Presenting and explaining a law, theory, or postulate

♦ Asking students what they know and want to know about the new topic

♦ Posing a problem or question without allowing time for students to ponder or discuss it, or immediately giving the solution or answer to the question themselves

In almost all of these situations, students receive information without the opportunity to mentally engage in the learning process. In some of these situations, the teacher expends a great deal of energy in planning and presenting information meant to gain students' attention or motivate interest. In reality, however, how effective are these strategies?

In most of the situations described above, the teacher is usually unaware of what each learner brings into the learning environment. There is no way to know what the learners are thinking, or what connections they are making between their prior experiences and the information presented.

What occurs in Commit to a Position or an Outcome?

What does "commit" imply? The dictionary gives some definitions that provide insights into why this phase of the lesson is important to the learners. These definitions include "to put in charge;" "to reveal the views of;" or "to pledge." These terms appropriately express what we would like to see happen during this phase of the lesson. During *Commit to a Position or an Outcome*, students are given a challenge and put in charge of their learning. To respond to the challenge, students are asked to discover and reveal their own views or thinking about the pertinent concept(s) and where their ideas originate. We then want them to commit or pledge to keep thinking until they can make better sense of the concepts.

During this phase of the lesson, the major responsibility for learning is placed on the learner through immediate and active engagement in a carefully designed task. This phase involves the student in the learning process in a meaningful and deliberate way, as they are encouraged to draw upon their own personal experiences to respond to a challenge posed by the teacher. Hence, by mentally "grabbing" the learners, the teacher stimulates a motivation to pursue the question or problem at hand.

Student dispositions we hope to see

When we pose a beginning challenge and ask students to write their ideas, we hope to see learners who are willing to:

- ◆ Think deeply about things
- ◆ Think about what they understand
- ◆ Reflect on their own experiences

- Become aware of their own thinking
- Write down their beliefs in regard to the challenge, committing to a point of view

Because this first phase of the lesson is critical to the effectiveness of the entire lesson, we must think about the appropriateness and effectiveness of the question or problem. The challenge establishes an environment that sets the stage for students to:

- Develop conceptual understanding
- Develop skills
- Develop desirable dispositions

What are some appropriate strategies?

In many of their writings, the authors have referred to this phase of the lesson as "Commit to an Outcome." That is because the CCM was originally developed for science instruction, and the usual first step was to ask students to **make a prediction** about something. As numerous teachers from diverse content areas have worked with the model, it has become clear that a prediction is not the only means of engaging students in the content. What's important is to provide a question or problem that requires the learners to think about what they know and understand in order to respond. At this first phase of the lesson, the learner makes a personal and private commitment in response. Making a prediction is only one of several strategies.

For most students, privately **writing** or **drawing** a picture is an effective method for making a commitment. **Manipulating physical objects** can also be effective if you have enough materials for every student. For very young learners with limited writing skills, you may also consider asking them to sit and "**think quietly to themselves.**"

Numerous strategies are appropriate for students to *Commit to a Position or an Outcome*, depending on the content and learning expectations:

- Identifying and recognizing patterns
- Sorting and classifying
- Comparing and contrasting
- Making predictions
- Estimating

♦ Judging a claim

♦ Determining an intent

♦ Making an inference

♦ Interpreting information from an example (*e.g.*, map, written passage)

♦ Making a conjecture

♦ Proposing a theory

♦ Taking a position on a dilemma

♦ Creating or interpreting an analogy

♦ Suggesting a problem-solving strategy or procedure

♦ Creating a mental model (drawing or constructing an image of the student's mental representation of a phenomenon that is too small to see, too large or distant to effectively observe, or abstract in nature)

How do we plan this phase of the lesson?

Some strategies work better than others—one size does not fit all. Making a prediction works well for many science experiences. Dealing with a dilemma often works well for interdisciplinary experiences. Identifying a pattern can work for many content areas, including mathematics, music, language arts, and the sciences.

Deciding which strategy to use or how to pose a challenge is often seen as the most difficult aspect of creating a CCM lesson. Focusing clearly and explicitly on what we want the students to learn will aid immensely in this aspect of planning.

Here is an example. National and state standards all have benchmarks pertaining to students' understanding of the attributes of geometric shapes. Why is this important? What do we want them to understand? Recognizing attributes of objects is one way in which we come to understand how things are classified. From our earlier discussion, you may recall that being able to classify things is important to developing and applying conceptual understanding.

For this concept, a logical strategy for opening the lesson might be to provide students with cutouts of two-dimensional shapes and ask them to **classify** the cutout shapes by posing the following challenge: "Divide these geometric shapes into groups and explain how you decided on the groupings." Inviting students to classify objects provides them the opportunity to think of various attributes and to discover that there are many ways to categorize things.

Thinking about commonly held misconceptions is another helpful consideration in deciding how to pose a challenge for *Commit to a Position or an Outcome*. Consider illustrations and physical models that are commonly used to represent intangible situations—for example, for very small objects such as atoms and molecules and very large-scale topics or phenomena, such as the solar system, seasons, or day and night. Our work and that of others have revealed that many students develop misconceptions when they think in terms of the models that are used to represent these abstract or intangible concepts.

An effective way to remedy this problem is to challenge students to use their own observations and experiences to build **mental models** that represent their understanding of the phenomena. Throughout the later phases of the lesson, they can modify and improve their models to reflect their maturing understanding. Having students construct their own models is often an improvement over giving them commercially prepared models, which do not give students the opportunity to learn about the process of model building and the reasons for having models.

For many teachers, deliberately thinking about how best to confront student preconceptions in the next phase of the lesson provides the guidance and creative energy needed to think through this phase, as well as the entire lesson. Some teachers find it helpful to conceptualize the manner in which students will confront their beliefs before structuring an appropriate challenge for them to *Commit to a Position or an Outcome*. Other teachers find that thinking about how to challenge students' thinking in the *Commit to a Position or an Outcome* phase leads them naturally to the development of the remaining phases of the lesson. There does not seem to be one correct approach, as long as clear learning expectations for the lesson are kept in mind.

The following are some examples of ways in which a teacher might invite students to *Commit to a Position or an Outcome*. As you read each of these examples, think about the content addressed, the misconceptions that might be targeted, the strategies being used, the mental activity required by the students, and how the students' ideas might be tested.

♦ "Draw a picture of a human circulatory system, with arrows to show the direction in which blood flows to and from the heart. Explain your logic."

♦ "If this globe represents the Earth, which of these spheres could represent the Moon? How did you decide?"

♦ "Look at the cover of the book I'm holding. Write down what you believe is going to happen in this book. Give your reasons."

♦ "You have 755 feet of gift wrapping paper. If you need 63 inches of paper to wrap each gift, how many gifts do you estimate you could wrap using the paper you have? Without making calculations, explain how you arrived at your estimate."

♦ "There are 30 seconds left in the first half of the basketball game and the score is tied. Would you use a zone or man-to-man defense at this time? What are your reasons?"

♦ "You have just finished dinner in a nice restaurant. How many strategies could you use to determine a tip equal to 15% of the bill? How did you come up with these ideas?"

Detailed planning examples

The following examples represent how we approached developing some challenges for the *Commit to a Position or an Outcome* phase of the four sample lessons (Appendix I). We will follow the development of these same lessons through each of the next five chapters.

Community planning

Recognizing the complex issues involved in community planning is important to all our citizenry. Determining the environmental impacts of our decisions and then deciding on how much weight to give those impacts are real-life skills.

To introduce a unit or lesson on this topic, I decided to present students with a dilemma and challenge them to **take a position** by considering the pros and cons of the problem at hand. The following is the challenge I will pose:

"The state has proposed building a power plant by the river. The plant has the potential to create numerous jobs for the community. There are, however, indications that it may affect the air and water quality of the surrounding region. Considering the economic and environmental impacts, should the plant be built? Why or why not?"

This lesson opening will provide opportunities for my students to recognize their own current understanding of the issues, as well as their values in relation to the environment and economics of a community. In the remaining phases of the lesson, students will have rich opportunities to gather information, examine and weigh issues, and go through the complex processes involved with making a community decision. As students complete the lesson, they will have opportunities to reassess their understanding of the issues, as well as the foundation for their value judgments.

Density

I want my students to learn about density and factors that may cause things to sink or float in water. Many students come to class bringing intuitive ideas that things sink because they are heavy and float because they are light. I want my students to experience that "very heavy things" may float and "very light things" may sink. Although students may have **covered** the concept of density, memorized definitions, and even calculated densities in the past, they may not have had experiences that provide sufficient motivation to let go of intuitive or naïve conceptions.

I believe that asking students to **make predictions** about which items will sink or float will provide an excellent opportunity for students to draw on their personal experiences and **uncover** what they know about floating and sinking. I will provide a set of objects and ask students to make their predictions. The items I select for this will represent a range of sizes, shapes, and weights to get students to ponder and reflect on their experiences to determine what they understand, what they are uncertain about, and where their ideas originate.

Making predictions provides a great opportunity for students to get excited as they anticipate what will happen because, if chosen carefully, some objects would not be immediately obvious. For example, a watermelon that weighs 10 kg and a bean that weighs 2 gm will provide unexpected results. I have noticed that many students love being challenged to make predictions and can't wait for the opportunity to test their ideas.

Word recognition

In listening to students read, I noticed that many students tend to have difficulties deciding whether the letter "c" will have a soft "s" sound or hard "k" sound when they are decoding new words. I want them to have an experience that will help them develop an understanding of how our language works, so they can become more independent and confident in their reading.

I will provide students with a list of words containing the letter "c" in various positions. Some of the words will be familiar to the students, but most will be nonsense words. I will ask students to **sort the words into groups** based on the sound the "c" makes and to write down how they decided where to place each word. Completing this classification activity will make students aware of any strategies they currently use; alternatively, they will recognize whether they simply guess at the letter sound in unfamiliar words.

Understanding pi

Many college students can state that *pi* is approximately 3.14, but despite exposure to geometry many do not know what *pi* represents. They can solve problems involving *pi*, such as finding the area and perimeter of circular objects or calculating the volume of 3-dimensional shapes. Many students, however, do not know that *pi* is a ratio of the circumference to diameter of a circle. Nor have they seen *pi* expressed as 22:7 or 22/7.

I will challenge my students by presenting the claim that regardless of the size of a circle, the ratio of the distance around to the distance across is always the same. I will then ask them to **judge the claim** as true or false and give their reasons. Judging the claim will involve students in thinking about their understanding rather than making computations with memorized formulas.

How do we facilitate Commit to a Position or an Outcome?

Challenges made during *Commit to a Position or an Outcome* should be brief and immediately call upon the learners to draw on their own thinking, with minimal distractions or intrusion on this individual process. Because this is a private process, individuals cannot simply go along with their friends or participate invisibly in "groupthink."

Role of the student

In the *Commit to a Position or an Outcome* phase of the lesson, the learner works independently and actively as he or she:

◆ Responds to the challenge

◆ Writes down predictions, personal views, or answers to questions

◆ Provides a rationale for own ideas

◆ Becomes aware of own ideas

◆ Takes time to make connections and draw on personal experiences

◆ Recognizes gaps in own understanding

Role of the teacher

As this phase of the lesson is facilitated, the teacher:

◆ Presents a challenging question or problem

◆ Provides time for students to reflect on the challenge

◆ Creates a safe and inviting environment for students to reflect on their previous experiences

◆ Allows students ample time to think about and write down their views

What common problems occur in planning and facilitating this phase?

As educators first endeavor to create and facilitate CCM lessons, they may experience some common problems. These are likely due to the fact that the CCM is radically different from traditional instruction (Chapter 1). One of the reasons for writing this book is to help teachers develop enough understanding of the model to be able to apply it effectively. Since we are unable to converse with you as you plan your lessons, we thought it might be helpful to share some of the common difficulties people encounter in their early CCM experiences.

The following practices are things that should be avoided:

◆ Posing more than one question

◆ Directing students' thinking by the manner in which the question or challenge is presented

♦ Implying that the teacher is looking for a particular answer or rationale

♦ Suggesting that specific information or experiences should be drawn upon to respond to the challenge

♦ Posing questions that are not directly related to the concept or skill to be targeted

♦ Posing questions focused on students' likes or interests, such as "How many people like pizza?"

♦ Presenting lengthy, rambling scenarios

♦ Posing low-level, factual recall or comprehension questions

♦ Having the students actually complete the entire activity during this phase

♦ Treating this phase as a separate activity

♦ Posing questions that the teacher answers herself or himself

♦ Collecting, critiquing, or grading students' written commitments

Putting ideas on paper can be difficult for some students, and students can be very concerned about committing ideas to writing. This reluctance usually stems from a fear of being wrong. It is very important that students understand that you will not collect, review, or evaluate their notes from this phase of the lesson. The willingness to *Commit to a Position or an Outcome* is an important disposition for open communication and learning.

> As learners, we need to be able to risk being wrong or we risk not learning.

What do we assess during Commit to a Position or an Outcome?

During this phase of the lesson, the teacher should be relatively invisible as students spend time individually accessing their personal experiences and ideas that will help them respond to the challenge. This phase of the lesson affords the teacher the opportunity to identify the comfort levels of students in making a written commitment. If the CCM is a new process in the class, this can be easily observed as the teacher visually surveys the class from a distance.

If the students are already comfortable with the CCM format, the teacher can casually circulate around the room without interacting with students. During this time, the teacher may unobtrusively observe and take notes on the types of responses that students are recording. This information may be helpful in leading the group discussions during the rest of the lesson.

Teachers' comments about Commit to a Position or an Outcome

♦ "It gives students the opportunity to think on their own and become personally involved in the activity and the outcome."

♦ "It makes students more responsible for things. It teaches students to be more confident."

♦ "The new challenge creates an excitement and curiosity for students."

♦ "I make my students use a marker or crayon for their predictions. I want them to learn it is OK not to have the correct answer. I want them to be excited about exploring math."

♦ "I love this phase because it is so telling. I can use students' journal entries as 'interviews' and know what misconceptions they have."

♦ "My students like this part. They like making predictions and aren't afraid to be wrong."

♦ "It helps kids draw on their knowledge and stretch a little, also."

♦ "The phase is great! Predicting sets the stage. Wording the challenge question is very important. Be sure to clarify that students understand what is being asked."

♦ "It makes students take a stand or position."

♦ "It can be a hard step for fear of being wrong. However, it gets easier the more students do it."

♦ "It gives ownership and helps students become <u>aware</u> of their own thinking."

♦ "Getting students to write down their beliefs provides opportunity for their ideas to be looked at and later confronted."

CHAPTER 4: EXPOSE BELIEFS

What is the purpose of this phase?

If we think about our own classroom experiences as students, we might recall that there were always a few students who jumped to answer questions or provide solutions to problems posed by the teacher. It seemed that these students were always taking notes, nodding their heads, and raising their hands. These were the same students called upon whenever the teacher wanted to hear the correct answer. Everyone regarded them as the smart kids.

Other students did not seem to have much to contribute in class, and of course, there also were a few students whom everyone considered as not too bright. These students quit trying. They did not complete assignments or answer questions in class. We may have heard them refer to themselves as stupid or dumb. On occasion, teachers and other students reinforced those ideas.

If we were not among the smart group, we might have doubted our own abilities and intelligence. Our feelings of inadequacy in these classroom settings may have stemmed from the fact that we were restricted to the information and views provided by the teacher and textbooks. We usually only heard the correct or official definitions of terms that represented complex concepts. There were not many opportunities for us to learn what our classmates thought or to become aware of diverse ideas that existed about any given topic. We seldom had the opportunity to reflect on our own thinking or that of our classmates. At times, we may have felt that we were the only ones who did not understand something.

Hearing others' ideas helps students realize that classmates have ideas similar to or very different from their own. The process, referred to by Vygotsky (1978) as "social transmission," provides students with awareness and accepting attitudes about the views, ideas, and experiences of others. This awareness can be a tremendous relief for some students and help protect their self-esteem.

What occurs in Expose Beliefs?

In the environment created in CCM lessons, students share their ideas and listen to the ideas of others. Although these may be different from those of the teacher and textbooks, they are valued and considered important. Students recognize that they also have permission to have different views, as they uncover their own preconceptions and those of their classmates. In CCM lessons, the classroom is a place where students come to reflect safely on their views and become aware of the views of others. We believe this exemplifies the characteristics of a true learning community.

In the *Expose Beliefs* phase of a CCM lesson, students are reminded and encouraged to share their ideas, without fear of not knowing the right answer. Everyone is able to share ideas without being judged. As students participate in later phases of the lesson, they have opportunities to judge the quality of their thinking and revise their ideas as they work with materials, collaborate with classmates, and gather new information.

During this phase of the lesson, students initially share their ideas in small groups, then a representative from each group shares everyone's ideas with the whole class. With younger students, however, it may be appropriate to share only in small groups or only in the large group, depending upon the activity and students' attention spans.

The ideal situation for the small group sharing of beliefs involves students working in groups of 4 or 5 to record all their ideas and reasoning. One group member may be appointed to write down the ideas of every member of the group. This may be done using chart paper and markers, or as some teachers have suggested, with overhead transparencies for later display with the entire class. In the primary grades, children may prefer to have their own corner of the paper on which to write or draw.

Students are taught to listen respectfully without making judgments, criticizing, or vetoing any of the views and ideas presented. As students gain experience with the model and become comfortable sharing ideas, they begin to interact more during this phase, asking their peers for further explanation, challenging each other's thinking, and at times debating ideas. These are healthy, intellectual activities, as long as they are conducted respectfully.

It is important to note that a group consensus is not sought, and students should be informed that they can change their ideas. As they listen to one another's reasons, and as they are asked to explain their ideas further, students may find themselves changing their minds about their beliefs. This is a logical, acceptable, and desirable learning practice. When we recognize our ideas or logic as faulty, we should change our thinking.

Working in small groups provides a safe environment for students to take the risk of sharing and exposing their ideas, rather than immediately sharing them in a large group. This large-group sharing occurs in the second part of *Expose Beliefs*, and involves bringing all the ideas in the class together. After recording their ideas, the members of each small group select one member to present their ideas to the entire class.

Students should be encouraged to do this without identifying the source of each idea. This anonymity helps maintain a low-risk environment. It is very important that no one feel embarrassed during the process. We encourage students to simply say, "These are all the ideas from our group." However, as ideas are shared by the presenter, other group members may clarify comments that may have been misrepresented or add information that may have been overlooked. If the teacher deems that primary students should only share in small groups, he or she should take a few moments to summarize the ideas heard while circulating through the class, so students have the opportunity to hear a variety of ideas.

This phase of the lesson provides a great opportunity for students to develop respectful communication skills, as they share their own thinking and listen to others' views. They learn from and about their classmates. Many students involved in CCM lessons have said that as a result of listening to their classmates, they have come to develop a new appreciation for others and their ideas.

Student dispositions we hope to see

During the *Expose Beliefs* phase of the lesson, we should expect to see students:

- ♦ Thinking about their own and others' ideas
- ♦ Willing to share their own views and rationales
- ♦ Demonstrating respect and consideration for each others' ideas
- ♦ Interested in listening to others' views
- ♦ Willing to rethink their own ideas
- ♦ Feeling confident in the nonjudgmental environment created by the teacher

What are some appropriate strategies?

Depending on the topic and level of the students, the manner in which ideas are shared may vary. Strategies for *Expose Beliefs* in small groups might include having students:

- ♦ Create a list of each person's ideas and rationale
- ♦ Make a two-column chart to list predictions or ideas with corresponding reasons
- ♦ Draw pictures to represent each student's ideas
- ♦ Create a group tally sheet
- ♦ Illustrate each person's problem-solving strategy
- ♦ Draw diagrams representing pattern extensions or classification groupings

How do we plan this phase of the lesson?

As in the previous chapter, deciding the exact manner in which students should expose their beliefs will depend on the concept being addressed, along with the strategy that was used during *Commit to a Position or an Outcome*. Using the examples from Chapter 3, we provide some specific examples of how students might use the above strategies to share their ideas in small groups.

- ♦ "Draw a picture of a human circulatory system, with arrows to show the direction in which blood flows to and from the heart. Explain your logic."

    - Each group has been given an outline of the human body. Members of the group should use different colors to draw their ideas of how blood flows to and from the heart and other parts of the body.

- ♦ "If this globe represents the Earth, which of these spheres could represent the Moon? How did you decide?"

    - Create a list of everyone's ideas and rationale.

- ♦ "Look at the cover of the book I'm holding. Write down what you believe is going to happen in this book. Give your reasons."

    - Create a master list of story ideas and write a sentence describing the clues each person used to form those opinions.

♦ "You have 755 feet of gift-wrapping paper. If you need 63 inches of paper to wrap each gift, how many gifts do you estimate you could wrap using the paper you have? Without making calculations, explain how you arrived at your estimate."

- List everybody's estimates and their strategies for making them.

♦ "There are 30 seconds left in the first half of the basketball game and the score is tied. Would you use a zone or man-to-man defense at this time? What are your reasons?"

- Draw a diagram for each defense and list all the reasons members of the group used to support their choices.

♦ "You have just finished dinner in a nice restaurant. How many strategies could you use to determine a tip equal to 15% of the bill? How did you come up with these ideas?"

- List all the ways of finding the tip the members of the group came up with and their reasons for proposing them.

Detailed planning examples

Community planning

I want to give students the opportunity to share their positions on whether or not the power plant should be built and give reasons for their positions in small groups. In order for them to see the pros and cons of the situation, I might have the students create a two-column chart with titles signifying the positions **Build** or **Not Build**. At the top of each column, they might record the number of students who take each position. Then they can list all of their reasons supporting each view. As they develop these lists, students will begin to recognize a variety of factors that must be considered in making such a complex decision. As students continue in later phases of the lesson, they may decide to expand these lists to include more factors they deem important.

In a lesson such as this, I expect some strong feelings or emotions to surface because of students' previous experiences or conversations at home. At the beginning of this phase of the lesson,

I will provide some instruction about the importance of respecting the views of others.

As students share their group ideas with the whole class, I will also remind them that all members of their group have the opportunity and right to clarify their positions. I expect a rather lively discussion here and will need to guard against criticism and judgmental attitudes.

Density

During this phase, I will have each small group select one member to write down all the predictions and reasons on a large sheet of chart paper. If more than one student has the same prediction and rationale, they can make tally marks to indicate this.

While students are working in small groups, I will quietly observe and write notes to myself about things to take into account as the lesson proceeds. I will be especially alert to ideas that relate to variables other than the ones I expect to see them testing in later phases of the lesson and must think about how these should be discussed later in the lesson. I may recognize the need to gather additional materials.

Word recognition

I expect that the small-group sharing of the ways in which they classified the words containing the letter "c" will help the students become aware that they used a variety of strategies. They will also recognize that they have differing ideas about where to place the nonsense words. As there is likely to be little or no agreement on these strange words, any concern about knowing the pronunciation of these words should disappear.

As students compare their lists, it will help them to list all the strategies they used to sort the unknown words. Asking a member from each group to share their group's methods for classifying the unknown words with the whole group should reveal numerous strategies and generate great curiosity about how to figure out which sound the letter "c" should make.

Understanding pi

I will ask students to work in groups to share their beliefs on the conjecture that all circles have the same ratio of circumference to diameter. It is probably best to have students first share the number of true and false votes in the group. Then, they can have a member of the group record all the reasons for each true or false vote on chart paper. Having one person share the group's vote totals and list of reasons with the entire class will give us an opportunity to record and display for the class the vote totals and the variety of reasons used to support student ideas.

How do we facilitate Expose Beliefs?

When facilitating this phase of the lesson, the teacher provides opportunities for students to discuss their ideas safely, in small and large groups. Whether students share their ideas only in small groups or in large groups, the teacher should summarize the ideas presented without revealing any judgments about students' views. This is to ensure that everyone has the opportunity to see his or her ideas and views represented fairly.

As students work in small groups, it is important that the teacher walk around the room, listening, observing, and noting the ideas and questions students articulate. This information will be important in facilitating the whole group discussions in this and later phases of the lesson.

Role of the student

As students work to *Expose Beliefs*, they will:

- ♦ Share ideas and views in small groups
- ♦ Listen and carefully consider each person's views and ideas
- ♦ Question other students if ideas are not clear
- ♦ Reflect on their own understandings
- ♦ Change their views and ideas if convinced their thinking is flawed
- ♦ Discuss ideas respectfully as they gain experience in the process

Role of the teacher

During the *Expose Beliefs* phase, the teacher will:

- ♦ Allow every student and group of students the opportunity to share their views and ideas
- ♦ Encourage students to respect the opinions of every student without making judgments

♦ Provide necessary materials (such as paper, markers, and tape) for groups of students to write down their ideas

♦ Record or summarize group responses without judgment or elaboration

♦ Ask for clarification of terminology students use

♦ Give students the opportunity to change their ideas

♦ Identify students' misconceptions to be addressed later

What common problems occur in planning and facilitating this phase?

As ideas are shared, the teacher and other students may ask clarifying questions, but it is critical that the teacher not make positive or negative judgments about any ideas. The teacher simply acknowledges students' ideas and thanks them for sharing their views. If the teacher hints that one idea may be very good, other students may feel deflated or feel that their thoughts are not as good as those being praised. Positive comments can be as destructive as negative comments in this setting. Praising behaviors is usually a good idea, but praising opinions may backfire. We should respect each other's rights to opinions as they are a result of our experiences.

Some things that we discourage include:

♦ Expectations that students come to consensus in their groups

♦ Students judging or criticizing the ideas of others

♦ Teacher judging students' ideas

♦ Teacher interrupting students as they present their ideas

♦ Teacher elaborating on students' comments

♦ Teacher providing an answer or solution to the lesson's question or challenge

What do we assess during Expose Beliefs?

As students are sharing their ideas, the teacher should walk around and listen to the ideas being presented and the level of discussion taking place within each group. It is at this time that the teacher gains awareness of the students' preconceptions and insights into where these ideas originate. Making notes of these discoveries will be of great value in (1) deciding whether the lesson is effective in changing conceptions, (2) refining the lesson, and (3) deciding what other lessons might be needed to address some strongly held naïve conceptions or misconceptions.

As in *Commit to a Position or an Outcome*, the teacher also has the opportunity to assess students' willingness to take the risk of sharing their ideas in small groups. In addition, the teacher may note how willing students are to consider alternate possibilities.

Teachers' comments about Expose Beliefs

- ♦ "Sharing helps students validate or question their individual ideas."

- ♦ "Students learn to respect others' ideas."

- ♦ "I like the way students share ideas with each other—this gives them the feeling that they are not alone."

- ♦ "Sharing is a great way to talk about and to hear other theories and ideas."

- ♦ "Most students participate and learn from each other's thinking and responses. Explaining their reasoning is great but tough sometimes."

- ♦ "This is where I believe a lot of learning takes place. Students learn to listen to one another and support one another's ideas."

- ♦ "Students have the chance to voice their thinking while also listening and learning from others—students have to analyze and rationalize their thinking."

- ♦ "I like that students get to share ideas with each other before sharing with the large group."

- ♦ "This phase can be a bit intimidating. Making predictions can be difficult at first. But, sharing with a partner or small group makes it feel a little more comfortable."

- ♦ "This phase of the lesson promotes risk taking, social skills, and creative learning, but it takes time."

- ♦ "This is the fun part of CCM. I want my students to feel free to explore ideas—to be able to work together like in real life."

- ♦ "It is important for students to share and take risks, listen to others' ideas and reasoning, and verbalize their thoughts."

CHAPTER 5: CONFRONT BELIEFS

What is the purpose of this phase?

When the mind is comfortable with its version of a concept or is following one path of logic and suddenly new information is received that is counter to the current thinking, the mind recognizes the conflict or dissonance and enters a state of confusion. According to Piaget (1964), this state of disequilibrium provides the optimal time for learning. This is because the mind is constantly adjusting toward a state of balance or equilibrium. When the mind recognizes dissonance it can dismiss the new information or it can find a means to resolve the conflict by reconciling old and new information. Through this process, the mind revises theoretical assumptions and understandings of the categories of information we call concepts.

During the first two phases of CCM instruction, learners may begin to experience dissonance as they initially think about their own ideas and listen to other people's ideas. In *Commit to a Position or an Outcome*, learners often recognize that their understanding is limited, but this does not necessarily create dissonance. However, as they begin hearing others' views, they are likely to encounter different ideas about the concept in question. At that point, learners may assume that others are wrong, assume they are wrong, or begin questioning the foundation upon which their ideas are based.

What occurs in Confront Beliefs?

During the *Confront Beliefs* phase of the lesson, we want to provide an experience that will allow the learners to recognize whether their ideas and initial logic paths make sense. To achieve this, students are placed in an environment that actively challenges and tests the positions they have taken and shared during *Commit to a Position or an Outcome* and *Expose Beliefs*. Having had the opportunity to think deeply about their own ideas and hearing those of their classmates, they are typically full of questions and curiosity.

The first two phases of the lesson are critical in this process. If the learner is not first aware of personal beliefs, there really is no opportunity for recognizing dissonance. The second phase, *Expose*

Beliefs, lays the groundwork that determines whether the learner accommodates or dismisses the new information encountered in the *Confront Beliefs* phase. The discussions that occur during the exposing of beliefs help create the desire to know. We postulate that learning requires thinking and usually only occurs when there is a **need to know** or a strong **desire to know**. The first two stages of the CCM help the learner enter that need-to-know or desire-to-know state of mind.

Creating dissonance in *Confront Beliefs* is not really difficult. Once the learners are in the pre-dissonant state, teachers need only provide an opportunity for learners to access information that is contrary to their beliefs. This direct, personal encounter with experiences that yield new information stimulates the internal struggle to accommodate it.

Student dispositions we hope to see

During this phase, we expect to see positive attitudes and willingness on the part of learners to:

◆ Think about the concepts

◆ Participate in exploring a problem

◆ Consider the complexities of the concept

◆ Discover and consider multiple possibilities

◆ Engage in intellectual dialogue and debate

◆ Recognize and admit their own confusion and misconceptions

◆ Take responsibility for their learning

What are some appropriate strategies?

There really is no end to the types of activities that can be used to help students confront their beliefs, recognize that their ideas and beliefs may not be sound, and experience conceptual change. As one might expect, some strategies are more conducive to this than others.

In general, strategies that provide an active role for the learners are better than strategies that place learners in the passive role. It is important to understand that it can be very difficult for someone, such as a teacher, to determine whether learners are mentally active unless they are involved in discussion. Strategies in which students are interacting with each other provide opportunities to judge the depth of thinking. This does not mean that students might not be mentally active during a lecture or while watching a video. It is just more difficult to discern this. Moreover, when direct instructional presentations are lengthy, there is a much greater opportunity for students to slip into passive or inattentive states.

Physical activity is not the only criterion we should consider when thinking about the quality of instruction at the *Confront Beliefs* phase of the lesson. As any teacher or parent can tell you, students can be very physically active without doing much thinking. Likewise, there are numerous mental activities that do not lead to thoughtful understanding; therefore, it is important to consider the cognitive level of the activity as well.

Examine the instructional strategies that follow to identify those that you feel are most effective for *Confront Beliefs*.

Passive Strategies

- Lecture
- Video
- Computer slide presentation
- Teacher demonstration
- Direct instruction with minimal interaction
- Teacher-explained model
- Teacher-explained classification system
- Teacher-explained diagrams

Active Strategies Requiring Low-level Cognition

- Follow a pre-designed experiment
- Textbook reading
- Flash cards
- Drill games
- Drill worksheets
- Creating mnemonics
- Memorization songs
- Closed-ended questioning
- Guided practice for learning specified procedures

- Labeling models and diagrams
- Computer-assisted instruction (CAI)
- Completing pre-designed classification charts

Active Strategies Requiring Higher-level Cognition

- Student-designed and -conducted experiment or field study
- Guided problem exploration
- Inventing a procedure
- Compare and Contrast
- Strategy game
- Research paper
- Open-ended questions
- Student-developed graphic organizers
- Student-developed models
- Creating and testing patterns
- Shared Inquiry process for literature discussions
- Two-column note taking
- Student-developed classification systems with justifications
- Simulations

Did you decide that active learning strategies involving high-level cognition are probably the best for CCM lessons? We believe they are probably best suited for CCM lessons, but we also know that those active, high-level cognitive activities may not be possible with all content. A few of the strategies listed as requiring low-level cognition could be completed with a high-level of cognition, just as many of the strategies listed as passive could be mentally active for some learners.

There are some instances in which passive instruction works well and is appropriate. However, low-level cognition is probably never appropriate for a CCM lesson. If the goal of instruction is only to memorize or recall information, the CCM is not the best choice.

We might also argue that a limited number of things should be learned strictly by memorization.   When we bring this up with parents and teachers, they frequently argue that things such as multiplication facts and phonics must be memorized. We agree, but we will also suggest that there are concepts associated with these facts and rules that need to be developed. Through patterning and classification strategies, students have the opportunity to learn basic facts while developing the concepts.

How do we plan this phase of the lesson?

In general, concepts that can be represented concretely should involve **physical exploration** during *Confront Beliefs*. Topics in physical, life, earth, and environmental sciences, as well as many areas of mathematics, have numerous concepts for which students can develop increased understanding through hands-on, minds-on activities. Physical strategies can also work for aspects of other content areas, including music, social studies, and physical education.

Many topics in other areas, such as social studies, literature, and chemistry, may not appear as content for which physical activity is possible or appropriate. For such topics, we need to think about whether concepts can be represented graphically or through simulations. As described in Chapters 3 and 4, having students **draw diagrams** is a good method for identifying their preconceived notions about things that are not easily observable. How then, do we have students confront their beliefs about such difficult concepts? In some instances, we can have them explore ideas using materials that will **simulate** the concept. For example, students can get some useful information about the phases of the moon or the seasons by using a light source and spherical objects.

Many concepts are easily observed at certain times or with sophisticated equipment, but may not be available to you or your students. These situations may also be appropriate for simulations. For example, some activities in *Project Wild* (www.projectwild.org) offer **physical simulations** that can be used to explore population trends among animal groups over time. **Computer simulations** can be used to explore the effects of social interactions, and **mathematical models** may offer opportunities to examine historical trends.

What about understanding the symbolism in a piece of literature? The question posed in the *Commit to a Position or an Outcome* phase of a literature lesson should stimulate discussion that will compel students to read or re-read the work. As they search for passages to support their contentions, they will ponder the author's intent and possible interpretations.

Reading is a skill that we take for granted, but it is also an essential strategy to think of in relation to CCM lessons in all areas—not just literature. Textbooks and other written and computer-based reference materials can be excellent resources for student exploration. After students become aware that they need information during the *Commit* and *Expose* phases of the lesson, providing resources may be all that is needed for learners to effectively confront their beliefs for some topics. These resources can be supplemented with expert lectures or video. The point is to provide sources of information that will allow students to investigate or research information.

After students have completed the planned activities during *Confront Beliefs*, we do not expect complete understanding. In fact, we expect more questions from students. If they are in a state of disequilibrium, you will find that they are actively thinking and really trying to understand. The lesson does not end here. They need time to *Accommodate the Concept* (revise their theories and assumptions) and make personal sense through making connections (*Extend the Concept)* and posing new questions and ideas *(Go Beyond)*—the rest of a CCM lesson.

Detailed planning examples

Community planning

I want students to consider the factors they have identified as relevant, and then determine what other information they would need to help them decide to build or not to build the power plant. Rather than give them a text or direct them to specific resources, I want them to learn how to become independent in identifying resources. Therefore, I will ask them to list ideas about where to locate information. As they are working on this, I will visit each group, talk with them about their ideas, and provide some feedback about the quality of resources they selected. If the situation warrants, I may stop and have a whole-class discussion, asking questions to help students think about what constitutes a **good** resource for this project.

Based on what the groups decide, I will assist in locating and gathering resources to save time and provide opportunities for students to access the information they need. The resources may include websites, journals, and outside experts. As the students work, they should sort their findings in support of or opposition to the proposed project. Each group might be instructed to plan arguments in favor of both positions. This will further motivate students to confront and reconsider their personal views.

Density

After listening to all ideas during *Expose Beliefs*, I want students to return to their small groups to discuss what they have heard and to propose a plan for testing their predictions, including identifying the materials they will need.

Even though students are planning the procedures, I need to anticipate what they might reasonably request. For example, I need to have all the items on the prediction list plus a variety of other objects of different shapes, sizes, and densities. I can expect that students may want to weigh and measure items, so I will also bring in a scale, graduated cylinders, and other measuring devices. I will also need a clear container, such as a small aquarium or plastic shoebox, for each group to fill with water to test which items will sink and float. Since I included a watermelon in the prediction list, I will also need a large clear container, such as an aquarium or large plastic storage bin.

I would like students to decide, in their groups, what observations they need to make, what kind of data to collect, and how to organize and display their data. I want them to gain confidence and independence in this, so I will try to ask questions to help guide the process, without telling them what to do and how to do it.

When the tests are concluded, I want members of the group to compare their results with all the predictions that had been made. Recognizing or confronting any conflict between the predictions and the observations is a crucial piece of the experience. As students struggle with unanticipated results, they will experience what Piaget and other scholars refer to as disequilibrium, or cognitive dissonance. It is this direct, internal conflict that helps the learners become aware of a need to change and expand their thinking.

Word recognition

I want my students to recognize there might be a way to figure out which sound a "c" represents in a word without my telling them. I believe that if they struggle to figure it out, they are less likely to forget it. I also know they will be very proud of themselves and will gain confidence in their reading and thinking abilities.

To provide this opportunity, I will have them set aside the lists they created in the first two phases of the lesson. I will provide a sheet of paper with familiar words containing the letter "c" that have been divided into two lists, sorted according to the sound of the "c."

Without my telling them, students should be able to discover a means to determine when the "c" makes a hard or soft sound. To complete the task, I expect that they will examine the position of the "c" in each word, the letters that come before and after the "c," and some things I have not considered. When they share their ideas with others, we will probably find that their ideas are similar. This will reinforce that they are all smart and able readers.

Understanding pi

In this situation, I want students to test their ideas by measuring a variety of circles, then determining the ratios. I will require that they graph the relationship from each of their tests. This will provide a scatter plot that should help them see the consistency of the ratios. In order for them to understand what they are discovering with this hands-on activity, I want them to be as independent as possible. I will avoid telling them how to complete their measurements or how to set up their graphs, as I believe they need to think through that process to become proficient in these skills. I will remind them of the importance of labels and titles in helping the reader interpret their results.

Because measuring circles can be challenging, I will provide cans or jar lids, string, rulers, and measuring tapes. As students work, I will walk around the room asking questions to be sure they understand what they are doing, to redirect them if they are using inefficient or ineffective strategies, and to help them decide if their graphs are interpretable. I will be careful not to explain or direct because I want them to figure this out themselves. If they have results that are inaccurate, they will recognize this during the next phase of the lesson and have the opportunity to find and correct their errors.

How do we facilitate *Confront Beliefs?*

The level of cognition used during *Confront Beliefs* is a student choice, but the motivation is usually stimulated by an effectively implemented CCM lesson. Traditional educational practices often lead students to believe their role in the learning environment is merely to remember information. A CCM lesson requires much more from the students—students must think continuously.

During *Confront Beliefs*, students should be comparing what they are experiencing with what they previously believed. If we do a good job of designing the lesson, students will be asking themselves and each other "why" and "how" questions as they work. At this phase, learners should be thinking deeply about the content. We expect them to be mentally struggling to understand. We might even see some signs of frustration as the learners discover they cannot yet make sense of what they are experiencing. This is especially true of students who are comfortable and successful with traditional instruction and memorization.

Many high-performing students in traditional classrooms are confident in their ability to obtain high grades by reading the text, answering questions on the readings and classroom experiences, and taking tests. As they progress through the CCM lesson, these students may experience uncertainty, which can be upsetting if they begin to fret about their grades. You may hear them complain and ask you to explain what they are "supposed to be learning." Once students have been through a few CCM lessons, most realize that they are learning far more than they would have learned through traditional instruction and eventually come to value the process.

During the *Confront Beliefs* phase of the lesson, the teacher's role in the activity is probably more passive than the students' role. Teachers spend most of the time facilitating student investigation. The teacher should provide what students need, and observe, listen, and ask questions but not interfere or interrupt the lesson to explain concepts. Facilitating this stage of learning means allowing exploration, standing aside, and providing students with a bit of freedom and independence. This is not as easy as it sounds. We may see students heading down a wrong path or struggling to find a procedure for solving a problem. Our natural tendency is to jump in to show them or help them. In doing so, we rob them of the opportunity to understand why some things don't work.

Student errors are important to understanding, so we should resist the temptation to get them back on track immediately. Having said this, we can assist, without directing them, by simply asking questions that require students to explain why they are doing what they are doing. Often, a simple question such as, "Why are you using that material?" or "Why are you looking for that information?" will help students recognize their errors. If they stop to explain, they must stop to think, too.

Role of the students

As students work, their role is to:

♦ Test their ideas
♦ Explore
♦ Experiment
♦ Observe
♦ Collect data or information
♦ Seek additional resources
♦ Design and redesign
♦ Ask questions of each other
♦ Discuss their procedures
♦ Discuss their data or information
♦ Collaborate with teammates
♦ Do their part in the group's work
♦ Explore multiple solutions, strategies, or perspectives

Role of the teacher

During the *Confront Beliefs* phase of the CCM lesson, teachers spend most of the time facilitating student investigation. The teacher:

♦ Provides opportunity for student decision making
♦ Provides resources or facilitates access to resources
♦ Monitors the environment
♦ Provides guidance in conflict avoidance and resolution
♦ Ensures safety procedures are followed, if warranted
♦ Asks clarifying questions
♦ Encourages independence

♦ Responds to questions with questions to help learners think through their dilemmas

♦ Allows some opportunity for students to struggle

♦ Allows students the opportunity to recognize and correct their errors

♦ Responds to their thinking without judging

What common problems occur in planning and facilitating this phase?

Most of us are probably accustomed to providing careful instructions for what the students should do and how they should do it, because that is the way most of us were taught. While this is appropriate for some CCM lessons, we should try to avoid that routine practice when it is not needed, letting students design their own plans. Some additional common problems to be avoided include:

♦ Designing activities that lead to learning one specific procedure or way of doing something

♦ Designing activities that require one specific, correct answer

♦ Leading students in one pre-determined direction

♦ Asking questions that imply the teacher is looking for a specific response

♦ Expecting students to use one skill or procedure

♦ Designing activities that require only low-level cognition

♦ Designing activities that are actually guided or independent practice of a skill

What do we assess during this phase?

Everything that occurs during the *Confront Beliefs* phase of a CCM lesson provides the teacher with rich opportunities to learn about students' understanding. It is important to circulate, observe, and ask questions throughout this phase of the lesson, but do so to understand how students are thinking or to help them reconsider their processes, not to redirect their thinking to align with yours.

Observe the way students interact. How do they solve problems and make decisions? How do they work as a team? Does each individual participate and at what level? Does each person fight for the right to be included? Do they listen to one another? Do they show respect for everyone's ideas?

Discover how students think. Ask questions that will help you gain insight as to how students are making sense of their work. Listen carefully to their conversations. Are they recognizing important factors in the problem? Are they following logical paths? Are they willing to change directions when they recognize errors? What types of connections are they making? Are they relating this experience to previous knowledge and experience? Are they staying focused on the challenge or pursuing another interesting path?

The information gathered during this phase of the lesson will be helpful during the discussions that follow in the final three phases of the lesson. It will also be helpful in revising the activity for the future, planning follow-up lessons, and generally accommodating the learning styles and needs of your students.

Whenever possible, take notes. Impressions may last, but the specifics needed for future planning may be lost without some documentation. As in a Chinese proverb famously quoted by Benjamin Franklin, "The palest ink is better than the brightest memory."

Teachers' comments about Confront Beliefs

◆ "Students are sometimes proven wrong, but they learn so much through the hands-on experiences, rather than me lecturing."

◆ "Kids are able to test their theories."

◆ "This step makes learning stick!"

◆ "Students have fun solving the problem or figuring out the answer."

◆ "This challenges students to try their ideas and others' ideas to eliminate misconceptions."

◆ "Finding out if their theory was correct is great. Students may feel somewhat insecure if their ideas were incorrect, but figuring it out is a big aha!"

◆ "Students enjoy working together to test their predictions."

◆ "Always the best part of the lesson!"

♦ "This is the actual 'doing.' Testing out their predictions can be very exciting for students!"

♦ "It is important for students to be able to figure out the ideas and test them."

♦ "Everyone has ideas. This step allows students the opportunity to be an individual within a team, and learn to respect each other."

CHAPTER 6: ACCOMMODATE THE CONCEPT

What is the purpose of this phase?

After struggling with mental conflicts, collecting new information, and working with peers, learners need an opportunity to actively think about and make sense of what they are experiencing. During the initial three phases of the CCM lesson, learners acknowledged, shared, and challenged their entry-level ideas—all experiences designed to provoke cognitive dissonance.

It is important to provide time for students to continue thinking and talking as they begin the process of resolving their cognitive conflicts. Each learner needs the opportunity to develop a revised mental schema that incorporates the new information and experiences. Once this new organizational structure is developed, reflecting a more advanced understanding of the concepts that were explored, the learner's mind can return to a state of equilibrium.

Resolving mental conflicts can be challenging work. Try to think about times when you had to make sense of new experiences. Did you find yourself mentally redefining constructs or rearranging your image of how things fit together? Sometimes it is difficult to become aware of the thinking processes we use to accommodate new ideas and information.

It may be helpful to think about physical activities that involve reorganizing something familiar, such as computer files, a bedroom closet, kitchen cabinets, or the tools in your garage. How do you go about this? You initially recognize a problem that signals a need for re-organization. Something is not working or making sense. You might pause here in your reading and explore this metacognitively, listing the mental questions, processes, and activities you would undertake to complete the task.

While going through the process of accommodating new ideas and information, your mind works its way from disequilibrium— where there was a problem—to equilibrium, when you have developed a schema that satisfactorily accommodates all the information considered. In a learning environment, students must be asked to think about how new information fits or does not fit into their mental structures if we expect real learning to take place. As learners encounter information that does not fit, they need to be challenged to reorganize their mental schemas to accommodate the new information.

In traditional approaches to instruction, we assume students are making sense of the things they are hearing, reading, and doing. We assume they are accepting the new information, but we really do not know whether this is true. In fact, in traditional instruction, we operate on the premise that our role is to present information as part of the expert-defined structure of the system in which it exists. The thought is that if we present information carefully, explain how things are related to the system, and remind students of what we taught the day before, students will slowly build a mental structure identical to that which we present.

A major problem with these assumptions is that they exclude all of the learner's personal and individual experiences—the very things that the mind uses to make sense of new experiences and information. We do not know how each student's mind deals with new information. We do not know what the learners are thinking. Piaget notes that real learning does not occur unless the learners have the opportunity to accommodate new concepts. This means we must challenge them to do so. Some learners hear new information and simply dismiss it. It is our responsibility to see that this does not happen.

In traditional instruction, we believe that carefully building the logic for the learners will ease learning and prevent confusion. As we explain the rationale and structure of plant classification and taxonomy, for example, learners probably recognize the logic we present. We (and they) assume they are assimilating this new information into their existing knowledge structures. If we were to present a challenge requiring them to place an unknown species into the taxonomy, however, they might find that they really do not understand the system. The questions that would arise in their minds would trigger disequilibrium and the need to make sense of this system in relation to what they already understand and what they don't understand, but the lesson structure may not assist them in negotiating the deeper learning that is necessary. This is the point in traditional instruction at which the learners are left on their own. They may give up and accept their lack of understanding as the teacher moves on to the next topic, or they may find some way to make sense of the system on their own.

What occurs in Accommodate the Concept?

During the *Accommodate the Concept* phase, students are reporting what they have discovered, synthesizing their learning, and comparing it to their preconceptions. Our experiences show that as students struggle to understand and make sense of things in their own ways, they borrow and incorporate ideas from their classmates, the teacher, and from other resources.

The teacher is more overtly involved in orchestrating this phase of the lesson. The teacher actively assists students in the accommodation process by skillfully posing questions that help students sort through all they have discovered, prompting them to identify patterns and relationships in the data and information they collected. Teachers with advanced understanding in the field may have an easier time determining which questions are important to ask in order to assist students through the struggle. However, all teachers, regardless of their level of content understanding, can assist students by asking them to explain the "how" and "why" of their conjectures.

As this phase of the lesson is facilitated, it is a good idea to ask students if they want to alter their ideas based on what they have heard during the class discussion. This can be quite powerful and important. Students need to understand it is okay and expected that they will alter their conclusions as they gain new ideas and information. They are assured it is permissible to build on other people's ideas as they do this.

When the teacher recognizes that students have developed a satisfactory understanding of the concept, he or she may help them bridge minor gaps in their thinking by providing additional information, relating students' statements to those of the experts. This also is the time to provide appropriate vocabulary for concepts the students understand.

Accommodate the Concept is not the end of the lesson, and therefore, is not a time to close or wrap-up. Students still need to summarize and apply what they learned by coming up with their own examples and new questions in the later phases of the lesson. During this phase of accommodation, the teacher still needs to exercise some restraint in providing information and filling in the blanks for students.

If we find during the discussion that students are stuck on a particular factor or characteristic that is preventing them from fully grasping the concept, we may want to loop back through the model by posing a new question for students to work through before going on to the last two phases of the originally planned lesson. As stated earlier, this looping process is an appropriate strategy for dealing with complex or difficult concepts. (See Chapter 1.)

The *Accommodate the Concept* phase is largely collaborative, but we must respect the fact that accommodation is an individual and personal process and provide opportunities for all learners to explain their own understandings. This can often be accomplished following the group discussion by asking each learner to write an explanation or create a visual representation of the concept. This act mirrors the individual revelation of understanding during the *Commit to a Position or an Outcome* phase and helps students recognize how their thinking has changed as a result of the experiences.

As students and teacher become more comfortable with CCM lessons, the *Accommodate the Concept* phase can be quite interactive and exciting. Students may continue thinking about the concepts and challenging each others' thinking for extended periods of time by discussing their ideas with one another and the teacher, consulting resources, reviewing their notes, and repeating activity experiences. As they do this, they build positive learning dispositions and help each other come to a level of understanding that makes sense to each of them. When students are thinking in depth about complex concepts and phenomena, the teacher and students may even be thinking and discussing ideas on the same level.

We have stated that this phase of the lesson provides time for accommodation—a time for students to reorganize their mental schemas and a time for the mind to return to a state of equilibrium. Yet, we cannot realistically expect all conflicts to be resolved in the mind of every learner at the same time. The next phase of the CCM lesson—*Extend the Concept*—frequently helps, but in some instances students may still leave the classroom with unresolved conflicts. This may be disconcerting for some teachers, but we maintain that it is acceptable. Leaving with questions unanswered or conflicts unresolved is quite different from leaving with misconceptions. If learners leave the classroom with questions, they are likely to continue thinking and learning. As Bruner (1960) noted, "When the answer is given, learning stops."

Student dispositions we hope to see

During *Accommodate the Concept*, we may see students engaged in discussing, arguing, and debating. Of course, we encourage that this be done respectfully. Challenging each other's thinking in a learning community is healthy as long as students understand that they are challenging ideas and not people.

Things we hope to see among learners include:

◆ Willingness to think critically

◆ Willingness to consider the evidence

◆ Willingness to revise their ideas

◆ Willingness to formulate new ideas and theories

◆ Ability to admit confusion

◆ Desire to understand

◆ Confidence in their abilities to succeed

◆ Excitement about learning

◆ Persistence in effectively communicating results, conclusions, procedures, ideas, and conjectures

What are some appropriate strategies?

There are numerous ways to involve students in *Accommodate the Concept*. These can be group activities, but it is a good idea to provide opportunities for individual deviation from the group thinking. Student actions include:

◆ Participating in class discussion

◆ Developing a conjecture or theory

◆ Preparing a debate

◆ Inventing a procedure

◆ Presenting and interpreting data in a table or graph

◆ Creating a diagram or schematic

◆ Developing a fictional account

◆ Creating a model

◆ Making a presentation

◆ Explaining a solution or strategy

◆ Engaging in role playing
◆ Writing a summary or self-generated definitions of the main concepts

How do we plan this phase of the lesson?

Planning the *Accommodate the Concept* phase should flow quite naturally from the preceding phases. However, it is important to stay focused on the concept being addressed and the intent of the lesson. If our purpose is to help students understand division, for example, then we must give them an opportunity to explain the concept or describe their strategy for dividing and why it works. In this example, we should not expect one **right** method or one **right** definition. Rather, we should expect mathematically sound explanations. Asking questions and posing challenges are probably more effective instructional strategies than explaining errors because they require the students to recognize their own understandings, identify a conflict or dissonance, and work through accommodating information that does not fit with current schemas.

We must also consider what steps we might take if students' explanations are not sound or include misconceptions. Teachers frequently ask, "Should we just let errors go uncorrected?" At this phase, we may want to ask questions or present scenarios in which students can test their ideas to see if they are truly sound and recognize their own errors. Using the division example, let's imagine that students suggest that to divide any large number, you should just keep dividing it in half until you get the number of groups you want to make. You might give the students an opportunity to test the idea by asking them to make three equal groups from a group of 27 objects.

"Should testing of ideas be done in the *Accommodate* or *Extend* phase of the lesson?" is another question that frequently arises from teachers. There is probably not a right or wrong answer to this question because the phases flow together seamlessly. We typically provide an opportunity for testing during *Accommodate the Concept*. The *Extend the Concept* phase of the lesson is meant for students to make their own connections; however, ideas may also be tested in this phase. In Chapter 7, we will demonstrate how this may take place. The important point is that we allow the testing to occur.

Detailed planning examples

Community planning

At this point in the lesson, I want students to synthesize the relevant information they gathered and discuss the points they believe need to be considered as a result of their research. Each member of the group needs to be actively involved in this process, so I will ask each person to consider and reflect upon all the information and reconsider his or her position about whether or not the power plant should be built.

Group members might take turns communicating whether they have changed their positions, but I also want them to discuss this in a manner that I would expect to see in a County Commission meeting or public hearing. Then, I want a volunteer from each small group to present to the class a summary of the group's new understandings and positions, much the same way a committee might present their findings and recommendations.

I hope the class will then engage in a discussion to identify additional economic and environmental information that is needed to make a better or more informed decision. I will moderate the discussion and help to keep it focused on issues, problems, and solutions, rather than on which side wins. As needed, I will clarify definitions and processes that may be brought up. I want to know what each individual has learned from this experience. When the class discussion is finished, I will ask each student to write a paragraph summarizing her or his conclusions about the process of making a community decision.

Density

Dealing with the conflict between what students observe when placing solids in water and what they predicted is one of the important parts of this CCM lesson. I want to encourage and challenge them to come up with an explanation for what they observed. What is it that causes a small bean to sink, but a large watermelon to float?

During this phase of the lesson I want to give them the opportunity to borrow ideas from each other, consider the results of their experiments, and review their written resources to begin making sense of why things float or sink. Since this is rather complex, I may need to allow time for additional experiments before they are able to understand the relationships involved.

As students start to describe the relationships they recognize between volume and mass, I will use the opportunity to attach the correct scientific terms for the concepts they describe in lay terms. I might begin by simply asking if anyone knows what the concept is called. I know presenting definitions prematurely is often meaningless and can detract from students making sense of phenomena.

Word recognition

As a result of their exploration, the students should have figured out that the letter following the "c" is the determining factor for which sound the "c" makes. Now, I want them to develop a statement explaining this. Since we frequently use rules for coding and decoding words, I will ask students to work together to come up with one or more rules for deciding how to pronounce the letter "c" in an unknown word. I will ask each group to share all the rules they created and ask for clarification if statements are unclear.

To be certain that each individual has grasped the concept, I will ask each student to write an explanation of how to decide if a "c" is going to be pronounced with the "k" sound.

Understanding pi

I want students to recognize that all of the relationships they have recorded and plotted are very close to 3.14. Again, I don't want to over-guide them in the process. After they have reported and discussed their results, I will ask them to determine the decimal equivalency of each ratio recorded and determine the average—it may be that some groups already have done that, and it will be good to have the idea come from the students.

Once they have collected their data and completed their calculations, they can compare them, and I can ask them whether they recognize the results. This may be a good time to challenge older students to come up with a representation (other than a table) to display the relationship. As soon as they see the average, I expect they will recognize that the value is approximately the value of *pi*. I look forward to seeing their expressions. We will then discuss the question of why all those different-sized circles yielded the same ratio, focusing on the concept of ratio and the specific ratio of *pi*.

How do we facilitate Accommodate the Concept?

As students *Accommodate the Concept*, the teacher continues to act as a facilitator, encouraging students to make sense of their experiences in their own ways. In previous phases, the teacher wandered the room, observing, listening, answering questions, and helping students to maintain a collaborative environment.

In this phase, the teacher takes on a more direct leadership role in facilitating the lesson. He or she does this by guiding the class discussion, recording reported information, and probing for levels of student understanding, reasoning, and incomplete or incorrect conceptions. The teacher also helps students develop a more complete understanding, building upon what they have experienced during the lesson, including consulting textbooks and other references. Students are also given independent time to think and write.

Role of the students

During *Accommodate the Concept*, students:

♦ Relate the new information to previous knowledge
♦ Develop new understandings, ideas, and explanations
♦ Clarify their understandings
♦ Move towards resolving conceptual conflicts
♦ Borrow and incorporate ideas from their own observations and from other students
♦ Personally summarize their emerging understandings

Role of the teacher

In this phase of the lesson, the teacher:

♦ Asks students to collaborate in synthesizing their learning
♦ Provides time for students to discuss their ideas
♦ Allows students opportunities to share their results with the whole class
♦ Accepts all conjectures and ideas without judging
♦ Asks clarifying questions

♦ Asks probing questions to uncover what students truly think

♦ Provides appropriate vocabulary for the concepts students explain

♦ Answers additional questions students raise as a result of their efforts to understand

♦ Provides an opportunity for students to individually synthesize and express their learning

What common problems occur in planning and facilitating this phase?

Paradoxically, most errors or problems that occur during *Accommodate the Concept* result from the teacher's desire to make sure everyone understands the information in the same way and at the same time. This tends to arise from our traditional experiences in education, which lead us to believe that everyone should come away from a learning experience with a specific understanding or skill. Writing lesson expectations that focus on higher-level cognitive abilities will help minimize this.

The following represent things the teacher might try to avoid:

♦ Over-talking and over-explaining

♦ Creating a totally new or separate activity for this phase

♦ Explaining the concept to the learners

♦ Over-directing or steering students in a particular direction

♦ Signifying students' conclusions as right or wrong

♦ Providing examples of how the concept is applied elsewhere

♦ Expecting consensus

♦ Being concerned that everyone has not drawn the same conclusions

What do we assess during Accommodate the Concept?

As students are working to make sense of their experiences, the teacher has the opportunity to assess what students learned from the lesson, reflecting on several questions. "How have students progressed in the development of the specific lesson expectations?" "What additional information and experiences do they seem to need to meet these expectations?" "Do I need to loop back at this point to a new *Commit-Expose-Confront* experience for some concept or expectation that requires additional work?"

Individual progress can be measured by comparing students' understandings at this point with the views they expressed at the beginning of the lesson. Written statements, models, and graphical representations are examples of assessments that may be used during this phase. (See Chapter 9.)

The teacher should also make note of the dispositions exhibited during this phase. "Are students willing to dismiss prior ideas to incorporate the new information and experiences?" "Are they comfortable in expressing their thinking?" "Are they willing to defend their thinking and debate ideas with peers?" "Are they willing to change their thinking when logic and evidence warrant a change?"

Teachers' comments on Accommodate the Concept

♦ "By sharing, they can learn from someone else."

♦ "Allows students the chance to listen to a variety of ways a problem could be attacked."

♦ "The discussion after the experience helps students who often struggle."

♦ "At this phase, students who may not have a clear understanding have opportunity to listen to their peers to help their thinking."

♦ "Students can learn so much by sharing their views and ideas."

♦ "I love that students see their misconceptions and can explain how they changed their opinion and what new things they learned."

♦ "Helps students incorporate their new knowledge with their existing knowledge."

♦ "Many students have great ways of solving problems. They always teach me something new."

♦ "Students take their newfound knowledge and make it their own."

♦ "True conceptual change can happen. This is the most exciting part. This is the learning piece."

CHAPTER 7: EXTEND THE CONCEPT

What is the purpose of this phase?

Most educators place value on real-world applications of the content they teach. We believe that if students can see how the content is applied, they will understand it better. Therefore, teachers and textbook authors make a practice of providing examples of applications. Although providing examples is undoubtedly helpful to some learners, it is important that we recognize that these are the connections **we** readily understand. They may not have the same relevance to our students.

We recently witnessed the teaching of the concept of energy transfer in a university biochemistry course. In an effort to help students better understand the concept, the professor provided an explanation of how an internal combustion engine works, highlighting the oxidation and reduction reactions involved. Later, we had the opportunity to discuss energy transfer with the class and asked them to write their own explanations. Only one of the students referred to internal combustion engines, but most cited examples from a fermentation lab they had recently completed and their own biological systems. Some discussed the relationship at the molecular and cellular levels, while others discussed the applications at a system level, noting such things as body temperature regulation. However, each student had a unique way of explaining the process and making connections to the content and experiences with which they were most familiar. It should be noted that most of the students in the course were biology majors.

Constructivist theory and the research on misconceptions reveal that learners make connections to their previous experiences and understanding. Rarely, however, are learners asked to explain the connections they are making. This means there is a good chance the learner may not be very cognizant of the connections he or she is making. Moreover, for the most part, the teacher has little or no awareness of the connections students are making.

The lack of opportunity for learners to explain the connections they make means that they have relatively little time to reflect on the learning activity. Reflection time is important to consider multiple connections, as well as the strength and validity of the connections being made.

What occurs in Extend the Concept?

In the *Extend the Concept* phase of the lesson, the learners are asked to think about connections. They are asked questions such as: "Where have you seen this concept applied?" and "What experiences have you had where you have seen this?" and "What are some examples of this concept with which you are familiar?"

Rather than the teacher providing examples, he or she asks students to make connections and explain how the content is applied to real-life situations. Although this is usually done as a whole-class activity, individual students have the opportunity to reflect on the connections they see and consider the connections that their peers are making. Hearing one another's ideas can help students recognize even more connections and applications than they might think of independently. There certainly is opportunity to explore applications far beyond what the teacher might think to present.

It is quite intriguing to listen to students during this phase of the lesson. From our experience in teaching some lessons multiple times, we find there are common connections that students make as a result of the lesson experience, but inevitably there are new ideas that come up each time we facilitate the lesson.

It is also very exciting to watch students as they recognize connections. You can see their eyes light up and watch the "I got it" expression appear on their faces. During a week-long summer institute in science, we observed that one teacher participant seemed relatively unengaged during the first two-and-a-half days. She just didn't seem to have much interest. This was very odd, in that everyone else in the room was very actively involved. During the third day, we were facilitating an activity with pendulums. During the *Accommodate the Concept* phase of the lesson, participants began discussing center of gravity. As we moved into the *Extend the Concept* phase of the lesson, this young teacher nearly jumped out of her seat as she recognized a personal application of the concept. She began explaining how center of gravity is applied in dance, how shifts can affect spins, and so on. From that point on, she was one of the most enthusiastic participants in the institute. It was as if she suddenly realized that science was relevant to real life. The concepts have applications beyond the topic of discussion for the day.

This phase of the lesson, like *Accommodate the Concept*, can offer opportunities for students to test their ideas. For example, during *Accommodate the Concept* in a lesson on magnets, students may have conjectured that all metals are attracted to magnets. In addition to asking students to share examples of where these ideas apply or do not apply, it is sometimes important to allow students to test these application ideas immediately.

Student dispositions we hope to see

During this phase of a CCM lesson, we want to see students:

♦ Thinking about applications

♦ Being persistent in applying and connecting the concept to other areas

♦ Interested in hearing the connections their peers make

♦ Interested in understanding the connections others make

♦ Willing to recognize and change flawed thinking

♦ Interested in testing their new ideas

What are some appropriate strategies?

As in the other phases of the CCM, a variety of appropriate strategies can be used to get the learner to recognize how the concept is extended to other situations. The strategy that we use most frequently is simply to conduct a whole-group discussion asking students to tell us where else they have seen this applied. This and other strategies include:

♦ Asking the students to come up with familiar examples of the concept

♦ Having students individually or in a team make a list of ways in which they have seen the concept applied

♦ Having students select one example of the concept or process and create a drawing to illustrate it

♦ Having students make a list of books or stories, in the case of literature, with a similar theme, plot, or other characteristic

♦ In mathematics, having students show how their problem-solving procedures are applied to a different type of problem

- Having students make a list of the types of problems or situations in which their strategies could be used
- Having students create a concept map, illustrating the connections to different subject areas
- Having students identify careers in which the skill or concept would be useful or the professionals who would use it
- Having students explain the ways in which a particular decision or solution would have an impact on the system or related systems in the institution or environment

How do we plan this phase of the lesson?

Deciding which strategy is best suited for this phase of the lesson goes back to lesson intent, but other practical factors must also be considered. Time is always a big factor. As a teacher, you must weigh the benefits of doing something that requires drawing or writing against the time required for discussion.

The strategies used in the first four phases of the lesson will affect the decisions made in this phase of planning. Planning *Extend the Concept* involves identifying ways in which we can encourage each student to reflect again on prior experiences to make new connections and real-world applications of the concept that are personally meaningful. As in previous chapters, we present the logic we used in creating this phase of our four sample lessons.

Detailed planning examples

Community planning

After students have the opportunity to hear everyone's arguments and see the results of the vote, I want them to have time to reflect on two things. I want them to reflect on how they decided which way to vote on the issue. Did their votes reflect the logical arguments presented in class, or did they revert to their own personal values? I also want them to give consideration to how often public elections reflect careful intellectual consideration of the issues versus personal beliefs and values.

I also want my students to think about the fact that this seemed like a relatively simple decision until they got more involved in the process and recognized the complexity of the issue. I want them to think about community issues of which they are aware and try to determine whether or not any or all of the factors we considered in the power plant issue might be involved in these other issues.

An appropriate question might be, "What are some other community-planning decisions that might involve some or all of the factors we explored with the power-plant dilemma?"

Density

Coming up with examples or applications of how density affects whether things float or sink helps students connect what they are learning in class with the outside world. I want to challenge students by asking such questions as: "What are some other examples of what we have done?" "What are some applications of density?" and "How do we make use of these concepts in our daily lives?"

In addition to allowing and encouraging students to come up with the examples and applications of density on their own, I will be prepared to share some of my own examples.

Word recognition

It is important for students to think about whether their new rule applies elsewhere. I will ask students, "Are there other instances in which your rule will apply?" I suspect they will think about the letter "g" that also has a soft and a hard sound. If they do not suggest "g," I will ask them to consider it. I will also ask students to test their rule with "g" to see if it applies.

Since English is not only a language of rules, but also exceptions, I want students to determine whether there are any exceptions to the rule they created. I will ask: "Can you find any exceptions to your rule?" "What are they?" If time is insufficient for students to fully explore these questions, I will ask them to complete them at home with family members. Homework assignments like this are fun for students and provide wonderful opportunities for family members to be involved, maintain awareness of what their children are learning, and gain an understanding and appreciation for the instructional methods I am using.

Understanding pi

Now that students recognize the relationship of circumference to diameter as *pi*, I want them to think about the implications of this. I want them to think about how they could use this new understanding. I also want them to think about whether or not there may be other such standard ratios. Therefore, I will ask them direct questions, such as: "How can you use your understanding of *pi*?" "When might this come in handy?" and "Do you think there are other relationships like this?" "What might they be?"

How do we facilitate *Extend the Concept*?

The teacher facilitates the *Extend the Concept* phase by giving students an opportunity to further demonstrate and explain their understanding of the concept. Students are asked to identify and discuss real-world and content-related connections and applications.

Role of the students

As students *Extend the Concept* they are mentally and actively engaged in:

- ◆ Making connections to their daily lives
- ◆ Making connections to other real-world situations
- ◆ Making connections to other subject-matter content
- ◆ Clarifying their thinking
- ◆ Applying and testing procedures in new problems or situations
- ◆ Identifying and explaining procedural errors or conceptually flawed thinking

Role of the teacher

The teacher, although still a facilitator, is active in leading the discussion and prompting students to extend their understanding beyond the classroom. In this phase, the teacher:

- ◆ Asks students to share experiences where they have seen the concept or principle
- ◆ Challenges students to come up with examples
- ◆ Asks students to apply the concept to another situation
- ◆ Accepts students' answers without judgment
- ◆ Asks students to clarify the connections they are making
- ◆ Suggests own connections if none are identified by students

What common problems occur in planning and facilitating this phase?

During this phase of the lesson, problems can occur if:

♦ The teacher tries to get students to come up with a particular connection or application

♦ The teacher creates a whole new activity to get students to recognize and understand a specific connection or application

♦ The teacher views this phase as a traditional lesson "extension," trying to provide an additional task to extend learning to a new concept or related concept

♦ The teacher or students criticize or belittle the ideas that students present

What do we assess during Extend the Concept?

Assessing student understanding at this phase of the lesson is enjoyable and interesting, but can also present some challenges. Listening to students describe situations in which a concept is applied, we frequently hear similar applications. These are usually pretty obvious and tell us that students do indeed see appropriate connections. However, as students present new or unique applications, it is sometimes difficult to discern the connections they are making. We need to ask clarifying questions to try to determine whether the connection is valid or represents a misunderstanding.

At this point in the lesson, we occasionally see misapplications that result from an incomplete or somewhat skewed understanding of something discussed in the *Accommodate the Concept* phase of the lesson. Students can get stuck on an idea that they are trying to make sense of and carry that thinking through to this phase of the lesson. When this happens, you will recognize the mental struggle as they grasp for other examples to illustrate their thinking. During this phase of the lesson, some learners make a connection that will move them past the point where they were stuck on a flawed idea. Unfortunately, we have also seen an occasional student who is swayed by an inappropriate application suggested by a peer. When this happens, it is a clear indication that student understanding has not fully developed and there is a need to provide other resources or learning experiences.

Teachers' comments about Extend the Concept

♦ "This is important, to make it real for kids."

♦ "A good step for students to apply their knowledge at a higher level."

♦ "Students are able to relate concepts to real-life problems."

♦ "This stretches students' thinking as they tie their ideas to the real world."

♦ "This is fun for students. They walk into this step confidently."

♦ "To be able to apply their new knowledge somewhere else reinforces student learning. This makes learning stay with them."

♦ "It is so important for students to make connections to their world."

♦ "This can really excite students."

♦ "I'm always amazed by some of the connections kids make."

CHAPTER 8: GO BEYOND

What is the purpose of this phase?

Most teachers insist on having **closure** to their lessons, and the administrators, in evaluating their teachers, look for this in the lessons they observe. Teachers and administrators with this expectation believe that the summary and wrap-up at the end of the lesson is critically important. This is valued as the point of instruction where students hear all that they should have learned and defines what will later be tested.

It is our belief that emphasizing the notion of closure fosters students' beliefs and attitudes that there is finality to each lesson. In the minds of students, once that lesson closure takes place, all that was expected was accomplished, and they are ready to move on to something new. Whether or not students understand the concept by the end of the lesson is not relevant to them; learning stops and they do not consider that there is anything left to do or think about.

A CCM lesson begins with a challenge and ends with a challenge that frequently begins the cycle anew. It begins by challenging students to respond to a question, solve a problem, make a prediction, or build a mental model, for example. In *Go Beyond*, students are encouraged to think of new questions or problems to pursue that are related to the concept.

Encouraging and challenging students in this way gives the message that just because they have gone through a lesson and made some connections to the concept by thinking of examples, it does not mean that learning is finished. In fact, the message is that we have a new opportunity to **go beyond what has been learned** in a meaningful way. Some of the other phases in the CCM are used in a variety of forms in other models and by other researchers and educators. The *Go Beyond* phase, however, is unique to the CCM.

What occurs in Go Beyond?

In the *Go Beyond* phase, students are provided with new opportunities to think further about the concept. It opens new doors for creativity in posing and pursuing additional questions.

Some of the powerful questions that students generate during *Go Beyond* are of the "what if" type. Such questions offer great possibilities for students to pursue. The questions or problems raised by the students during this phase are genuine and come about naturally.

As students pose new questions, the teacher records these and asks how answers might be found. Many of these questions can be explored in class and used as the opening challenges for new CCM lessons. Some questions clearly need to be tested through further experimentation or exploration. For example, in the sample lesson related to *pi* students may ask how the ratio of circumference to diameter affects volume. This is a good question to be explored through further hands-on investigations. Other questions may be answered by seeking information. Questions such as "Who discovered *pi*?" or "Are there any power plants in our county?" can be answered by reading textbooks, searching the Internet, or talking with other people.

Of course, not all the questions or problems raised by students are possible or appropriate to pursue during class time. This, however, should not be an obstacle to allowing students to think about them. Student-generated questions may provide intriguing and meaningful opportunities for homework. Questions that are not important to conceptual understanding might merely be left for students to contemplate or explore independently, if they are interested in doing so.

As teachers will tell you, there never seems to be enough time in a class period to do all the things they would like to do. When time is an issue, the teacher may ask students to complete the *Go Beyond* phase of the lesson as homework, asking them to take time to reflect on their experiences and write meaningful questions that they feel would be worthy of pursuing.

The *Go Beyond* phase, unlike the emphasis on closure in traditional instruction, communicates to students that the more one learns about a topic, the more opportunities there are to question and to learn more. As students think about new questions, they often refer back to the discussions they had in *Extend the Concept*.

Student dispositions we hope to see

As students engage in the process of uncovering and stating their new questions, we see:

♦ Continued interest in the topic
♦ Willingness to ask new questions
♦ Interest in pursuing answers to new questions
♦ Increased curiosity
♦ Developing confidence in their abilities to pursue new questions
♦ Creativity and imagination

What are some appropriate strategies?

Strategies for *Go Beyond* are simple. We want to give students the opportunity to discover any remaining areas of confusion, think further about applications and connections, recognize and pose their own new questions, and consider how they may find answers. There are a few basic strategies that we use for this phase of the lesson. We ask students to:

♦ Pose their own new questions
♦ Identify things they would like to explore further
♦ Suggest ways in which they might explore the concepts
♦ Identify resources they might use to gather information

How do we plan this phase of the lesson?

Planning this phase is easy. We focus on the concept and probe to find out what questions students have and ideas they may be interested in pursuing. Our questions take the form of:

♦ What new questions do you have about these ideas?
♦ What new ideas do you have about how they may be applied?
♦ What new ideas or problems would you like to explore?
♦ How do you think you might find answers to your questions?

As we plan, we try to anticipate the kinds of questions students will ask in order to plan subsequent lessons. However, we are frequently surprised by the type and depth of questions that learners pose.

Detailed planning examples

Community planning

I want students to have time to recognize what other questions, problems, or concerns arose while working through this dilemma. Because this is a complex social, emotional, and intellectual problem, I suspect students will have many concerns and questions about the effectiveness of our political processes. I want to ask such questions as, "What new questions, problems, or ideas would you like to explore or discuss related to community planning or decision making?"

Density

I want to identify what questions or problems students would like to discuss and pursue. I especially want to hear what new lines of thinking have been stimulated. I will ask such questions as, "What are some other questions, problems, or ideas related to density that you would like to pursue?" Some students, depending on their levels and backgrounds, may initiate such questions as, "What would happen if we placed the solids in liquids other than water?" or "What can we do to make the sinkers float and the floaters sink?"

Word recognition

I expect that students will have questions about other rules for "sounding out" words or perhaps rules for spelling words. They might even wonder if they could use the rule they created for spelling. I believe it will be best to ask: "What questions do you have about what we did today?" and "Do you have questions about other rules we use in English?" I suspect our students for whom English is not their first language may have many questions that will spark interest in the English language among ALL of my students.

Understanding pi

This is an opportunity to encourage students to pursue new questions about pi, ratios, or related geometric relationships. I will ask the following types of questions to uncover these. "Do you have any other questions about *pi*, ratios, or geometric relationships?" "Are there other relationships you might like to test?" "What new ideas or problems would you like to pursue?"

How do we facilitate Go Beyond?

For the *Go Beyond* phase of the lesson to be successful, the teacher needs to relinquish power and allow the students to ask their own questions and pose problems important to them. The questions and problems generated by the students provide great opportunities for the teacher in planning a new CCM lesson. Doing this models for students how scientists, business people, and other professionals research and find solutions to problems and questions. This process models skills for continuous learning with which we hope all students will leave school.

We frequently find that the questions students raise during this phase of the lesson stimulate independent learning. Even if not assigned as homework, we find that students go home and test out ideas or research their questions using books, periodicals, and the Internet. The most rewarding and exciting results of this phase of the lesson are the conversations in which students engage their parents. Imagine when students go home from school and their parents ask them, "What did you do in school today?" Students respond with a lively description of the class activity and explain their understandings, theories, and ideas, then proceed to involve their parents in a lively discussion about their questions. Teachers using the CCM commonly receive phone calls from parents astounded by just such happenings in their homes.

Role of the students

As with the other phases of the CCM, *Go Beyond* emphasizes **uncovering new ideas** rather than simply **covering content**. As students are thinking about their questions, we expect them to:

◆ Think logically and creatively
◆ Continue to think about what they experienced
◆ Think about further applications
◆ Think about new possibilities
◆ Think about how they might test their new ideas
◆ Think about resources they might consult

Role of the teacher

During this phase, the teacher facilitates the process by:

◆ Asking for questions

♦ Providing opportunities for learners to recognize remaining confusion and questions

♦ Recording student questions and ideas for further exploration

♦ Providing opportunities for learners to continue thinking and learning about the concept and related concepts

♦ Providing encouragement and opportunity for learners to consult and use a variety of resources

♦ Asking for learners to suggest ways they might find answers

♦ Encouraging students to express ideas that go beyond what was done during the lesson

What common problems occur in planning and facilitating this phase?

Go Beyond belongs to the students. It is the time when they can think beyond the lesson expectations. They are still consciously and subconsciously assimilating and accommodating, so coming up with their own new ideas to explore is important. Some problems that arise are listed here.

♦ The teacher provides all the new questions and ideas to explore.

♦ Insufficient time is given for students to reflect and generate questions.

♦ Students are discouraged from thinking about certain areas of questions and problems.

♦ Students' curiosity is stifled with statements indicating that their questions are too advanced and that they will be addressed in later years or courses.

♦ Time is provided to discuss and explore only the easy and trivial questions and problems.

♦ Time is allotted to pursue every idea posed by students.

What do we assess during Go Beyond?

As we listen to students share their questions and ideas for further exploration, we should be listening carefully to discern what the questions and ideas reveal. Students' questions expose points of confusion and give us direct information about what they need to continue in their development of a more thorough or mature understanding. We want to learn whether students are using the new information gained from the lesson or if they are just dismissing it and reverting to their previous understanding. Are they asking questions related to the application of the skills and concepts that were developed in the lesson? Are they asking questions that reveal areas of confusion? Are they willing to pose questions of their own and propose new ways to use the information?

Teachers' comments about Go Beyond

♦ "Learning never stops! New questions spark new thinking and learning!"

♦ "This phase of the lesson is always useful."

♦ "This opens new doors. It can be considered a new learning and starting point, not the end."

♦ "This can be difficult for kindergarten due to their attention spans."

♦ "I like when we get to this. I do see some of my students taking it beyond, unfortunately with time constraints; I don't always do this step."

♦ "It gets students thinking about where to go next."

♦ "It has students use their new-found knowledge in other contexts."

♦ "I was feeling bad about not getting to this step, but realize it doesn't have to be done immediately. It's a great way to review the concept at a later time or to give as homework."

CHAPTER 9: ASSESSMENT AND THE CONCEPTUAL CHANGE MODEL

Assessment and evaluation

One of the most appealing aspects of conceptual change lessons is the opportunity to continuously investigate and keep track of student understanding. The lessons allow time for the teacher to make observations that help evaluate lesson effectiveness. We use the term **assessment** to refer to checking student understanding throughout the learning process. We use the term **evaluation** to refer to judgments about instructional effectiveness.

The CCM lends itself to numerous opportunities for continuous assessment of student development. Pre-assessment of student knowledge, understanding, and skills provides a starting point for lesson planning—including setting expectations—and helps the teacher create appropriate summative assessments. Formative assessments provide important information about students' dispositions, understanding of concepts, skill development, points of confusion, and abilities to communicate and apply ideas. Well-planned summative assessments provide opportunities for teachers to determine what students have learned as a result of their instructional experiences.

Likewise, the CCM lends itself to continuous evaluation and adjustment of instruction. It provides the teacher with opportunities for actively investigating, questioning, testing, and evaluating instructional strategies, materials, and curricular appropriateness. Because the teacher is not doing most of the talking during a CCM lesson, there are many opportunities to observe and listen to students as they work together and ask questions. Teacher facilitation of learning is responsive to the students and the situation.

Angelo and Cross (1993) summarize and give examples of kinds of assessments that are appropriate for specific learning situations. Their comprehensive and well-organized book has become a standard reference and the foundation for numerous assessment systems. It is a good resource for identifying assessments that are suitable for use with CCM lessons.

Pre-assessment

Importance and uses

Effective pre-assessments guide the teacher in identifying learning expectations, designing effective instructional experiences, and developing appropriate assessments aligned to expectations. One of the most dangerous and frustrating traps a teacher can enter is to assume that she or he knows what students already know and are able to do when they come to class. Just because a topic or skill was in the curriculum for a previous grade level, or because students were tested on it, doesn't mean they understand it. The limitations of these assumptions are underscored by the fact that students are increasingly mobile, curriculum standards and benchmarks vary from place to place, and the teacher cannot rely on knowing what and how a previous teacher taught—even in the same school.

Regular pre-assessments that are directly connected to what is about to be taught are both important and useful. The purpose of pre-assessment is to determine the students' honest entry levels before instruction involving a topic, concept, or skill; therefore, it should not be intimidating and should not be graded. It is an indicator—a baseline reference against which to assess ongoing progress.

Pre-assessment is not only for the teacher. Pre-assessments can help students develop their metacognitive skills as they identify what they know and how they know it. Metacognition is an important aspect of learning because it helps people understand their own learning styles, strengths, and difficulties in learning. It helps people dissect situations and problems with understanding, and to develop strategies and solutions that work best for them in various circumstances.

Some kinds of pre-assessment

Pre-tests

Perhaps the simplest and most common type of pre-assessment is an objective response pretest about vocabulary, facts, or skills. Although time-efficient, this is possibly the least effective way to measure what a student actually understands, because it focuses on information and procedures that have been memorized but that may or may not have been understood. Students who get high scores on such pre-assessments may have as poor a conceptual understanding as students who do not do well, and pre-test scores may be a misleading influence on the expectations of the teacher in preparing and presenting lessons.

Group questioning

Asking questions or brainstorming with the entire class is also popular. For very young children, this can be a useful and motivating process, as they have not yet learned to be self-conscious about volunteering their ideas and are excited to participate. This eagerness may gradually decline as students move through the grades if they experience judgmental reactions about their thinking from their teachers and peers. These large-group methods tend to favor students who are more confident in volunteering answers and ideas, while the thoughts of more self-conscious or reticent students (including those who feel they are "not good in school," "not good at math," or "have dumb ideas," for example) go overlooked.

Concept maps

Concept mapping is a sophisticated way for a person to reveal a personal, internal mental structure (conceptual framework) in regard to a topic (Novak and Cañas, 2006). Concept maps are both hierarchical and relational. The sample concept map shown here uses the same categories as the simple grouped hierarchy shown in Chapter 2—the original categories are in the boxes.

With a concept map, an individual reveals personal understanding about the relationships among things. These relationships are shown by drawing links with words that explain the perceived nature of the relationships. This feature distinguishes concept mapping from webbing, creating tree diagrams, outlining, or creating charts and lists. The example shown here can continue to grow, enveloping additional concepts that are related to the main idea of "household furnishings." Note that concepts incorporated in this example are related by structure, function, and even an ecological relationship. Where else might it go?

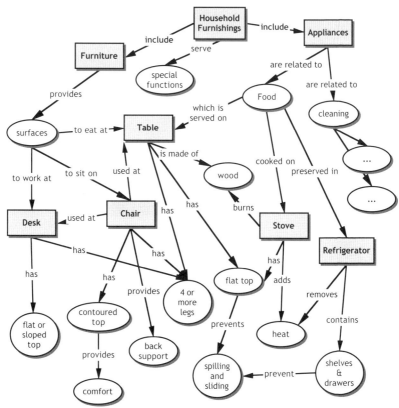

By looking at concept maps, an instructor can detect misunderstanding, needs for additional information and experiences, understanding that may be unique to an individual based on personal experiences, learner concerns or attitudes, or an unanticipated depth of understanding and ability to organize ideas. It allows for different cultural influences. It can be a guide for development of instruction and setting appropriate expectations for learning.

Creating a concept map is not a one-way street, because it causes others (*e.g.*, teachers, classmates, and colleagues) who examine it carefully to compare and test it against their own ideas. Nor is it used only for pre-assessment. It can open dialogue and be used to track developing student understanding. For example:

♦ After all members of a class have individually created their own concept maps, ask them to work in small groups to draw a composite, group concept map. They will learn from one another, and the activity can help them develop respect for diverse ideas and experiences. They can compare their group's concept map with those of other groups.

♦ Another strategy is to have individual students create a concept map prior to instruction, and then amend it with different colors of ink as they go along. This creates a visual reflection of their developing understanding.

The power of concept mapping has been demonstrated repeatedly. We would like to mention some cautions in using it for assessment, however. (1) Concept mapping requires a level of abstract thinking for which younger children are not ready. (2) When used as a pre-assessment, concept maps should not be graded, because they represent an individual, personal mental structure and are therefore correct and valid in terms of individual development and metacognition. (3) When used as a post-assessment of accomplished understanding, concept maps are very difficult and time-consuming to score objectively, although rubrics can be developed to analyze specific aspects. (4) Both making and reading concept maps require practice.

Interviews

Individual, structured interviews seem to be the most direct and reliable way to get a true picture of what a student understands and, by extension, the diversity of understanding that exists in a given class at a given moment. The process is discussed thoroughly in *Changing the Classroom from Within* (Stepans, Saigo, and Ebert, 1999), but here are some highlights.

As a prelude to designing conceptual change lessons, the teacher can conduct individual interviews with a handful of randomly selected students (*e.g.*, every 4th name in the class roster) on the concept or concepts to be taught. It is not necessary to interview every student in the class. The environment for interviewing should be private and free from distractions. The interview should be carefully designed. It is a good idea to test the process on a colleague, friend, or family member before using it with students.

Effective interviews often begin with a concrete situation or example to explore. Questions should be open-ended and lead to thoughtful probing with follow-up questions. They should not require simple recall of information, but should focus on asking the students to explain their answers; *e.g.*, "Can you explain a bit more about your thoughts?" "What are your reasons for that prediction?" "Why did you do it that way?" "Can you tell me what these numbers/words/methods represent and what they mean?" "Can you think of other, related ideas, possible answers, or ways to approach the problem?"

The interviewer should not coach or reward specific answers, and should not regard the interview as a "teachable moment." We need to be careful not to put words in the interviewees' mouths or attempt to rephrase their answers (*e.g.*, "So what you mean is..."). Tape-recording the interview allows the interviewer to focus on the interview and not on taking notes or trying to remember or analyze what is said, but needs to be done with absolute assurances of confidentiality. Above all, the interview should be comfortable, non-judgmental, and non-threatening, with the dynamic focusing on the importance of finding out what the interviewees have to say, in their own words.

Continuous assessment during a CCM lesson

Continuous assessment is part of the structure of a CCM lesson. Opportunities for assessment are embedded in each phase. Throughout the CCM lesson, students reveal their preconceptions, confusion, puzzlement, skill levels, competency, and developing understanding related to the concept, along with their collaborative and communication skills. Students are actively engaged with materials and in working with each other during most of a CCM lesson. As a result, the teacher has opportunities to observe, take notes, and make minor lesson adjustments. These observations are also helpful in planning further instruction.

We recommend that teachers formatively assess student progress on both dispositions and content throughout a CCM lesson. For the most part, only content-related skills, processes, and conceptual understanding are appropriate for summative assessment and grading.

The following sections present generic sets of expectations and corresponding rubrics for assessing dispositional and content expectations. These have been adapted from the expectations and rubrics found in *Targeting Students' Science Misconceptions* (Stepans, 2003).

Assessing dispositions

The following list of expectations contains some important dispositions that are commonly assessed during specific phases of a CCM lesson, as noted in earlier chapters, but most can be observed throughout a CCM lesson. These dispositions and the corresponding rubric contain items that may not be appropriate for every lesson. Conversely, the list is not all-inclusive, and teachers may wish to add dispositions they feel are important to the specific learning situation. Although not graded, assessment of dispositions can be helpful for planning and adjusting elements of the learning environment and for communicating with students, parents, other teachers, and administrators.

Sample expectations related to important learning dispositions

The student will demonstrate:

♦ Willingness to commit to a position or an outcome, identifying and explaining personal views in response to the challenge

♦ Willingness to share ideas and opinions

♦ Willingness to listen to others' ideas and opinions

♦ Willingness to confront ideas by testing them through new experiences

♦ Willingness to collaborate with others

♦ Respect for the opinions of others

♦ Willingness to initiate ideas and suggestions for carrying out tasks

♦ Willingness to revise ideas and beliefs

♦ Persistence in developing understanding

♦ Confidence in pursuing questions about the concept or topic

♦ Appreciation for the importance of the topic or concept

♦ Enjoyment and enthusiasm for challenges

Sample disposition rubric

Expectation targeted	Expectation met	Expectation developing	Expectation not met
Commitment to personal view in regard to the challenge	Willing to write down reasons or explanations	Makes some effort to write reasons or explanations	Resists writing reasons or explanations
Sharing ideas with group	Willing to share opinion and explanations	Attempts to share personal view and reasons	Resists sharing
Listening to ideas of classmates	Listens and considers others' alternate ideas	Shows some willingness to listen and consider others' ideas	Unwilling to give consideration to others' ideas
Confronting, testing personal views	Willing to test, confront ideas	Makes an attempt to test, confront ideas	Resists confronting ideas
Collaboration with group members	Collaborates effectively with others	Attempts to collaborate	Resists collaboration
Respect for ideas and suggestions of classmates	Consistently demonstrates respect for others' opinions and ideas	At times demonstrates respect for others' ideas	Demonstrates a lack of respect for opinions and ideas of some or all classmates
Initiative in presenting ideas, planning	Initiates and shares ideas	Attempts to initiate or share ideas	Does not initiate or share ideas
Flexibility and openness to new information and ideas	Willing to consider new information and revise ideas	Attempts to revise ideas	Unwilling to revise ideas

Persistence in completing tasks and actively thinking through the experience	Demonstrates persistence in completing tasks and thinking	Demonstrates inconsistent levels of persistence	Does not complete tasks or gives up easily
Confidence in pursuing questions	Demonstrates confidence throughout the lesson	Demonstrates confidence in some aspects the lesson	Demonstrates a lack of confidence
Appreciation for the importance and content of the topic	Demonstrates interest and enthusiasm	Demonstrates some interest or enthusiasm	Is disinterested, unwilling to engage
Excitement for responding to the challenge	Demonstrates interest and enthusiasm for exploring the challenge	Inconsistent in regard to interest and enthusiasm	Resists responding to the challenge and engaging in the associated learning

Assessing and grading content

Teachers learning about CCM lessons frequently ask questions about how to assess or evaluate students' understanding of the content, and subsequently how to grade that understanding. As in any instructional format or setting, such summative tools as **direct observations, paper-and-pencil tasks, projects, performance tasks, and student interviews** can be used appropriately and effectively with CCM lessons to assess and grade students' skills, processes, and conceptual understandings. Paper-and-pencil tasks may include written essays or reports, drawings, model development, various forms of data presentation, concept mapping, problem solving, and written tests. **Two-tiered assessments** [2] are particularly powerful and effective with conceptual change instruction (Treagust, 1988, 1995).

---

[2] A multiple-choice question designed to reveal misconceptions is followed up by an open question asking students why they chose their answer.

A key consideration is that assessments be directly aligned with the learning expectations and the instructional experiences that were provided for the students. For example, suddenly shifting to the end-of-chapter questions or prepackaged quizzes as a summative assessment is probably not a strong strategy; however, these resources may be a helpful source of ideas for writing questions that are adapted to the lesson. Since the CCM has consistently demonstrated that it opens opportunities for *all* students to achieve, it stands to reason that assessments should be consistent in attention to similar fairness and opportunities for students to express what they have learned in diverse ways.

The expectations listed below represent examples of content-based skills, processes, and conceptual understandings that may be written for some CCM lessons. These expectations are appropriate for summative assessment leading to grading. A rubric assessment would be used in conjunction with other tools for summative assessment and grading, as discussed earlier in this section.

Sample expectations related to skills, processes, and conceptual understanding

The learner will:

♦ Identify factors and variables that are critical to exploring or researching the problem

♦ Develop an appropriate plan for testing various ideas

♦ Conduct appropriate and adequate collection of information and data

♦ Accurately record necessary information and data

♦ Usefully organize information and data

♦ Search for and identify patterns, trends, and relationships

♦ Communicate data, information, and analyses using various modes (speaking, writing, tables, graphs, drawings)

♦ Extend, apply, and connect the topic to appropriate real-world situations and other academic experiences

♦ Pose new and creative questions, problems, or challenges directly related to the concept

♦ Demonstrate conceptual understanding and insight related to the topic

The rubric that follows correlates each sample expectation to quality indicators of skill and process proficiency, as well as indicators of conceptual understanding. Knowing what proficiency and understanding should look like will make the assessment and grading process more objective and effective. This sample rubric provides examples of how each of the above expectations might be assessed.

Sample content rubric for the above expectations

Expectation targeted	Expectation met	Expectation developing	Expectation not met
Identifies factors and variables related to investigating the challenge	Can identify and list multiple factors or variables that may be involved	Recognizes some of the factors or variables	Does not identify relevant factors or variables
	Identifies the information or data that needs to be collected	Identifies some of the information or data that needs to be collected	Does not determine what information or data needs to be collected
Develops plan for testing various ideas	Designs appropriate strategies and plan for exploring the problem	Strategy or plan has merit, but has flaws that may prevent successful exploration of the problem	Strategy or plan is inappropriate for the problem
Conducts appropriate and adequate collection of information and/or data	Identifies all potentially needed resources; locates needed resources	Identifies and locates some of the necessary resources	Does not determine what is needed and/or unable to locate resources
	Makes appropriate observations and/or measurements	Makes some appropriate observations and/or measurements	Most observations and/or measurements inappropriate and/or inaccurate

Accurately records necessary information and/or data	Accurately records notes, procedures, information, and/or data	Notes, procedures, information, and/or data are incomplete or recorded inaccurately	Does not record notes, procedures, information, and/or data to a substantive degree
Usefully organizes information and/or data	Able to sort and organize gathered information into logical sets and sequence	Demonstrates some logic in organizing related information	Does not demonstrate how bits of gathered information and/or data are related
Searches for and identifies patterns, trends, and relationships	Accurately identifies and explains patterns, trends, and relationships	Identifies some patterns, trends, relationships, but missing important considerations	Does not identify patterns, trends, and relationships
Communicates data, information, and analysis in appropriate form	Explanations and presentation clear, effective, and complete	Explanations and presentation partially appropriate, partially complete	Does not communicate clearly; format inappropriate for the situation
	Data, information, analysis effectively organized and communicated	Some difficulties with organizing and communicating data, information, analysis	Data, information, and/or analysis poorly or not organized
	Drawings, tables, graphs present data and/or information correctly and appropriately	Some visual representations successful; some inaccuracies in format and content	Rudimentary or no use of tables, graphs, drawings; problematic organization and choice of format

Extends, applies, connects topic to prior experiences and other contexts	Identifies and accurately explains connections and applications to real-world situations or previous academic studies	Identifies some loosely related connections and applications, that reveal incomplete or flawed understanding	Does not make connections or recognize applications
Poses new questions, problems, challenges to pursue	Poses new questions or problems that are germane to developing deeper understanding of the concept or related concepts	Volunteers ideas, but proposed ideas may have limited relevance to the concept	Does not pose new questions or problems that are related to the topic
Demonstrates conceptual understanding and insight	Synthesizes lesson experience and expresses understanding at appropriate level	Demonstrates some synthesis and partial understanding	Indications of synthesis and understanding are minimal or not present

Content expectations for the sample lessons

As we have emphasized, there should be alignment of expectations to assessments. Some specific content expectations for the sample lessons in this book are presented below. These are examples of expectations that can be effectively assessed and graded.

Community Planning

The learner will:

♦ Identify critical political, economic, social, and environmental factors to be considered in answering the question

♦ Develop a list of information and resources needed to prepare an argument for debate

♦ Accurately locate resources in the library, online, and in the person of professional experts

♦ Make accurate notes in an organized fashion

♦ Prepare a logical and coherent paper outlining the arguments supporting both sides of the issue

♦ Develop appropriate tables, charts, graphs, and statements

♦ Develop a persuasive essay in preparation for debate on the issues

♦ Write a critique of classmates' arguments following the presentations

♦ Develop a well-written paper indicating how each factor was considered in making a final determination on whether or not to build the power plant

Density

The learner will:

♦ Develop a plan for testing ideas

♦ Identify and control variables for mass, volume, and possibly shape

♦ Accurately measure the volume and mass of objects

♦ Create an appropriate table and graph

♦ Recognize and explain the relationships between volume, mass, and density

♦ Accurately calculate the density of a given object

♦ Develop an accurate explanation of how an object's density value is used to determine whether it will sink or float in water

♦ Give appropriate examples and applications of the concept of density

♦ Pose new questions and problems related to the topic of density

♦ Develop plausible explanations for why some very heavy objects might float

Word recognition

The learner will:

♦ Identify patterns in the lists of words provided

♦ Develop a logical method for sorting and classifying words on the lists provided

♦ Create a rule that can be used to determine whether the letter "c" will make a soft "s" or a hard "k" sound in the words provided

♦ Identify other words that follow the rule

♦ Identify exceptions to the rule

♦ Use the rule to correctly decode unfamiliar words containing the letter "c"

♦ Successfully apply the rule to the letter "g"

♦ Use patterning and classification skills to recognize and describe other word recognition and spelling rules

♦ Come up with new ideas of his or her own

Understanding pi

The learner will:

♦ Develop a plan for measuring diameter and circumference of various circular cylinders

♦ Accurately measure and record diameter and circumference values

♦ Organize and display the data as a table

♦ Accurately graph the relationship of diameter and circumference using appropriate scales and labels

♦ Interpret the graph

♦ Recognize and explain the relationship between diameter and circumference as a ratio

♦ Calculate the ratio 22:7 and its decimal equivalent

♦ Develop an accurate explanation of how changing one of the measurements would affect the other

♦ Give appropriate examples of how understanding the *pi* ratio might be useful in real-world settings

♦ Pose new questions or problems related to *pi* or other geometric relationships

Student self-assessment

Student self-assessments provide opportunities for students to reflect on the evolution of their own ideas, skills, attitudes, behaviors, understandings, and developing metacognition. Students' writing about an individual lesson or set of lessons on a topic may also provide the instructor with insights into how student dispositions and content understanding are developing, as well as the effectiveness of the lessons.

The following sample self-assessment prompts from Stepans (2003) are appropriate for students at various levels:

♦ The lesson was about [...]
♦ My initial thoughts and feelings about the lesson were [...]
♦ This is what we did in our small groups:
♦ My feelings about sharing my thoughts with others in the group were [...]
♦ The most difficult thing for me to do during the lesson was [...]
♦ My feelings during the activity were [...]
♦ I changed my thinking/beliefs with respect to [...]
♦ I changed because [...]
♦ This is how I now understand [the topic]:
♦ I would like to further investigate these questions or problems, or do a project about [...]
♦ This is how I feel about the value of studying [the topic]:
♦ Attached is a collection of my thoughts and work that I want to share.
♦ Other thoughts and reactions?

Evaluation of instruction

What assumptions do we make about the success of a lesson? Was it effective in helping students meet the lesson expectations or develop concepts and skills? If not, what could be done differently?

To some extent, lesson effectiveness can be inferred from student performance, but a deeper type of evaluation is a form of action research by the teacher. For this kind of classroom inquiry, teachers make and record organized, purposeful observations (Stepans, Saigo, and Ebert, 1999). Then they reflect on how they can use this research to better understand their students and the lessons.

Many teachers find it helpful to engage a colleague in such constructive evaluation, through peer observation or a three-question process. For the three-question process, the teacher asks a colleague to meet with students without the teacher present. The colleague randomly places the students in groups of three or four and asks each group to come to a consensus on all three questions regarding a lesson: (1) "What went well?" (2) "What did not go well and needs to change?" and, (3) "What are your specific suggestions for improvement?"

Teachers are also encouraged to share questions, ideas, and insights with colleagues. Many kinds of data can be collected for this purpose, including observation notes made during the lesson, student interviews, student performance results, and student surveys or feedback forms.

Assessment, evaluation, and continuous improvement

Teaching with the CCM is a dynamic process of continuous change and development. Students change in what they know, understand, and are able to do. Both students and teachers change as they become increasingly comfortable with the independent but purposeful atmosphere encouraged by the CCM. It may seem paradoxical, but it is by taking deliberate risks to expose and confront their own thinking and familiar habits that this comfort grows—in both students and teachers.

Assessment goes hand-in-hand with change. Measuring change requires multiple data points. To know where you are at any given point, you have to know where you started. The CCM provides opportunities for both teacher and students to be aware of students' developing understanding at multiple points in a lesson. It also provides rich opportunities for the teacher to collect data, reflect on these observations, and use this first-hand information to understand and evaluate what has happened to students in response to a lesson. It provides a basis upon which to improve instruction.

Ultimately, the CCM and the many constructive strategies that can be used within it help to create a deliberate and naturalistic environment of continuous development and improvement.

REFERENCES

American Association for the Advancement of Science. (1993). *Benchmarks for science literacy: A tool for curriculum reform.* New York: Oxford University Press.

Angelo, T. A. & Cross, K. P. (1993). *Classroom assessment techniques.* San Francisco: Jossey-Bass Publishers.

Atkins, M. & Karplus, R. (1962). Discovery or invention? *The Science Teacher, 29,*45-51.

Ausubel, D. P. (1963). *The psychology of meaningful verbal learning.* New York: Grune and Stratton.

Ausubel, D. (1968). Educational psychology: A cognitive view. New York: Holt, Rinehart and Winston.

Barnes, D. (1976). *From communication to curriculum.* Hammondsworth, UK: Penguin Books.

Bell, B. (1993). *Children's science, constructivism, and learning in science.* Geelong, Victoria, Australia: Deakin University Press.

Bonwell, C. C., & Eison, J. A. (1991). *Active Learning: Creating excitement in the classroom.* ASHE-ERIC Higher Education Reports. Washington, DC: Office of Educational Research and Improvement (U.S. Department of Education).

Boylan C. (1988). Enhancing learning in science. *Research in Science and Technological Education, 6*(2), 205-217.

Bransford, J., Brown, A., & Cocking, R. (Eds.). (2000). *How people learn: Brain, mind, experience, and school—Expanded version.* Washington, DC: National Academy Press.

Bruner, J. S. (1960). *The process of education.* New York: Vintage.

Bybee, R. W. and Landes, N. M. (1990). Science for life and living. *American Biology Teacher, 52*(2), 92-98.

Dewey, J. (1938). *Experience and education.* New York: Macmillan.

Diamond, M. & Hopson, A. (1998). *Magic trees of the mind: How to nurture your child's intelligence, creativity, and healthy emotions from birth to adolescence.* New York: Penguin Putnam.

Driver, R. and Oldham, V. (1986). A constructivist approach to curriculum development in science. *Studies in Science Education, 13,*105-122.

Duit, R., & Treagust, D. (1998). Learning science—from behaviourism towards social constructivism and beyond. In B. Fraser & K. Tobin (Eds.), *International Handbook of Science Education.* Dordrect, The Netherlands: Kluwer Academic Press.

Erickson, G. L. (1979). Children's conceptions of heat and temperature. *Science Education, 63,* 221-230.

Feuerstein, R. (1980). *Instrumental enrichment: An intervention program for cognitive modifiability.* Baltimore: University Park Press.

Gardner, H. (1983). *Frames of mind: The theory of multiple intelligences.* New York: Basic Books.

Glynn , S. M. & Duit, R. (Eds.). (1995). *Learning science in the schools: Research reforming practice.* Mahwah, NJ: Lawrence Erlbaum Associates, Publishers.

Hewson, P. W. & Hewson, M. G. (1988). An appropriate conception of teaching science: A view from studies of science learning. *Science Education, 72,* 597-614.

Hunter, R. (2004). *Madeline Hunter's mastery teaching: Increasing instructional effectiveness in elementary and secondary schools. Updated Edition.* Thousand Oaks, CA: Sage Publications.

Karplus, R., & Lawson, C. A. (Comps.). (1974). *SCIS teacher's handbook.* Berkeley, CA: Lawrence Hall of Science, University of Calfornia.

Karplus, R., & Thier, H. D. (1967). *A new look at elementary school science.* New trends in curriculum and instruction series. Berkeley, CA: Lawrence Hall of Science, University of California.

Karplus, R. (1977*). Science teaching and the development of reasoning.* Berkeley, CA: University of California Press.

Lawson, A. (1988). Student reasoning, concept acquisition, and a theory of science instruction. *Journal of College Science Teaching, 17,* 314-316.

Lawson, A. E., Abraham, M. R., & Renner, J. W. (1989). *A theory of instruction: Using the learning cycle to teach science concepts and thinking skills.* [Monograph, Number One]. Kansas State University, Manhattan, KS: National Association for Research in Science Teaching.

National Research Council. (1996). *National science education standards: Observe, interact, change, learn.* Washington, DC: National Academy Press.

National Research Council. (2000). *How people learn: Brain, mind, experience, and school—Expanded edition. J.D.* Bransford, A.L. Brown, & R.R. Cocking. (Eds.). Washington, DC: National Academy Press.

National Science Teachers Association. (2005a). *Exemplary science: Best practices in professional development.* Yager, R. E. (Ed.). Arlington, VA: NSTA Press.

National Science Teachers Association. (2005b). *Exemplary science: Standards-based success stories.* Yager, R. E. (Ed.). Arlington, VA: NSTA Press.

National Science Teachers Association. (2005c). *Exemplary science in grades 5-8: Standards-based success stories.* Yager, R. E. (Ed.). Arlington, VA: NSTA Press.

National Science Teachers Association. (2006). *Exemplary science in grades K-4: Standards-based success stories.* Yager, R. E. (Ed.). Arlington, VA: NSTA Press.

Novak, J. D. & Cañas, A. J. (2006). *The theory underlying concept maps and how to construct them.* Institute for Human and Machine Cognition at www.cmap.ihmc.us

Nussbaum, J. & Novick, S. (1982). Alternative frameworks, conceptual conflict and accommodation: toward a principled teaching strategy. *Instructional Science, 11,* 183-200.

Osborne, R., & Freyberg, P. (1985). Learning in science: The implications of children's science. London: Heinemann.

Osborne, R., & Wittrock, M. C. (1985). The generative learning model and its implications for science education. *Studies in Science Education, 12,* 59-87.

Osborne, R., & Wittrock, M. C. (1983). Learning science: A generative process. *Science Education, 67,* 489-508.

Osborne, R., Bell, B., & Gilbert, J. (1983). Science teaching and children's views of the world. *European Journal of Science Education, 5*(1), 1-5.

Piaget, J. (1964). Cognitive development in children: Development and learning. *Journal of Research in Science Teaching, 2,* 176-186.

Piaget, J. (1969). *The child's conception of the world.* Totowa, NJ: Littlefield, Adams and Co. (Originally published in 1929).

Posner, G., Strike, K., Hewson, P., & Gertzog, W. (1982). Accommodation of a scientific conception: Toward a theory of conceptual change. *Science Education, 66,* 211-227.

Project Wild. See www.projectwild.org

Renner, J. (1982). The power of purpose. *Science Education, 66*(5), 709-716.

Rowell, J. A. and Dawson, C. J. (1983). Laboratory counter examples and the growth of understanding in science. *European Journal of Science Education, 5*(2), 203-215.

Renner, J. W., & Marek, E. A. (1988). *The learning cycle and elementary school science teaching.* Portsmouth, NH: Heinemann Educational Books, Inc.

Rutherford, F. J. & Ahlgren, A. (1990). *Science for all Americans.* New York: Oxford University Press.

Rutherford, J. (1995). Hyphen-based reform. *2061 Today* (American Association for the Advancement of Science), *5*(1), 7.

Stepans, J.I. (1994). *Targeting students' science misconceptions: Physical science activities using the Conceptual Change Model* (1st ed.). Riverview, FL: Idea Factory, Inc.

Stepans, J.I. (2003). *Targeting students' science misconceptions: Physical science concepts using the Conceptual Change Model* (3rd ed.). Tampa, FL: Showboard, Inc.

Stepans, J. I., Saigo, B. W., & Ebert, C. (1995). *Changing the classroom from within: Partnership, collegiality, constructivism.* Montgomery, AL: Saiwood Publications.

Stepans, J. I., Saigo, B. W., & Ebert, C. (1999). *Changing the classroom from within: Partnership, collegiality, constructivism* (2nd ed.). Montgomery, AL: Saiwood Publications.

Stepans, J. I., Schmidt, D. L., Welsh, K. M., Reins, K. J, Saigo, B. W., & Kansky, R. J. (Ed.). (2005). *Teaching for K-12 mathematical understanding using the Conceptual Change Model.* St. Cloud, MN: Saiwood Publications.

Strike, K., & Posner, G. (1985). A conceptual change view of learning and understanding. In L. West & A. Pines (Eds.), *Cognitive structure and conceptual change.* Orlando, FL: Academic Press.

Treagust, D.F. (1988). The development and use of diagnostic instruments to evaluate students' misconceptions in science. *International Journal of Science Education, 10,* 159-169.

Treagust, D.F. (1995). Diagnostic assessment of students' science knowledge. In S.M. Glynn & R. Duit (Eds.). *Learning science in the schools: Research reforming practice* (pp. 327-346). Mahwah, NJ: Erlbaum.

Vygotsky, L. S. (1978). *Mind and society: The development of higher mental processes.* Cambridge, MA: Harvard University Press.

Yager, R. E. (1993). The constructivist learning model: Toward real reform in science education. *The Science Teacher, 60*(1), 53-57.

APPENDIX I. COMPLETE SAMPLE CCM LESSONS

Complete CCM lesson on Community Planning

Lesson level: Middle school to high school

Commit to a Position or an Outcome

The state has proposed building a power plant by the river. The plant has the potential to create numerous jobs for the community. There are, however, indications that it may affect the air and water quality of the surrounding area. Working individually, think about the potential economic and environmental impacts. Decide whether the plant should or should not be built and write down your reasons.

Expose Beliefs

With your teammates, make a two-column chart. Title one column "Build" and the other column "Not Build." List all the reasons your team has for supporting each position. Select a group member to share your ideas with the rest of the class.

Confront Beliefs

Return to your small group. Decide what further information you will need and where you can find it. Develop a research plan with your teammates. When you have completed your research, use the information you gathered to make a case for building a power plant and a case for not building the power plant.

Accommodate the Concept

In your group, decide which position you will recommend. Organize and prepare a presentation to make to the entire group as though you were a committee sharing your positions with the County Commission. Be prepared to defend your position. After all arguments are made, the class will vote on the issue. Finally, discuss the process with the whole class. How did personal beliefs and logical arguments influence your vote? Individually summarize what you have learned from this experience.

Extend the Concept

What are some other community-planning decisions that might involve some or all of the factors we explored with the power plant dilemma?

Go Beyond

What new questions, problems, or ideas would you like to explore or discuss related to community planning or decision making?

Complete CCM lesson on Density

Adapted from: *Middle to high school level lesson in Targeting Students' Science Misconceptions: Physical Science Activities Using the Conceptual* Change *Model*. (2003). J.I. Stepans. Tampa, FL: Showboard, Inc.

Lesson level: Elementary to middle school

Commit to a Position or an Outcome

You are given a small aquarium filled about 2/3 full of water. You also have such additional materials as: a grape, a bean, a potato, an ice cube, a bag of ice cubes (or block of ice), a small cube of modeling clay, a small watermelon, and a large block of modeling clay. On your own, predict what would happen to each item if you placed it in the water. Write down your predictions and your reasons for them.

Expose Beliefs

Share your predictions and explanations in your small group and summarize everyone's ideas on a large sheet of paper. Choose a spokesperson to share everyone's predictions and explanations with the entire class. After all the groups have shared ideas, decide whether or not you want to modify your own ideas before testing them.

Confront Beliefs

In your group, decide how you will test your ideas. Also decide what you should observe and record as you complete your tests. Then use the materials to test your predictions. Record your results as you work.

Accommodate the Concept

Work with your teammates to develop an explanation of why some things float and some sink. Based on your observations and the discussion, do you want to make any changes in your original explanations? Individually, write a statement describing your understanding of what causes things to float or sink in water and what density means to you. As you listen to the explanations of other groups, what are some new insights that you are developing about sinking, floating, and factors that cause solids to sink or float?

Extend the Concept

What are some other examples? What are some applications of density? How do we make use of the concept of density in our daily lives?

Go Beyond

What are some other questions, problems, or ideas related to density that you would like to pursue?

Complete CCM lesson on Word Recognition

Lesson level: Elementary

Commit to a Position or an Outcome

Look at the list of words provided. You will notice that they all contain the letter "c." Some of these are words you probably know. Others are nonsense words. The "c" in each of these words will make either a *soft* "s" sound or a *hard* "k" sound. Working individually, sort all of the words into two groups based on the sound the "c" makes. Think about the reasons you used to place each word in the soft "c" column or the hard "c" column.

Expose Beliefs

Compare your sorted lists with others in your group. Explain the reasons you used to sort your list. Choose one person from your group to share everybody's ideas with the class.

Confront Beliefs

Now look at the new list of words that has been sorted into two columns. These are all real words containing the letter "c." The words have been divided into columns based on the sound the "c" makes in each word. Work as a team to see what patterns or methods were used to sort these words.

Accommodate the Concept

Work together in your group to develop a rule you could share with others to help them determine when the letter "c" should make the soft or hard sound. Test it with other words that have the letter "c."

Extend the Concept

Does your rule work for any other letter that makes both a soft and hard sound? Can you find any exceptions to your rule? What are they?

Go Beyond

What questions do you have about what we did today? Do you have questions about other rules we use in English?

Complete CCM lesson on Understanding pi

Adapted from: *Teaching for K-12 Mathematical Understanding Using the Conceptual Change Model.* (2005) J.I. Stepans, D.L. Schmidt, K.M. Welsh, K.J. Reins, B.W. Saigo, R.J. Kansky (Ed.). St. Cloud, MN: Saiwood Publications.

Lesson level: Middle school to high school

Commit to a Position or an Outcome

Individually, look at the pictures or physical examples your teacher has provided of circular cylinders (when you look at them from the top, they are circles). Some people claim that regardless of the size of the cylinder, the ratio of the distance around the cylinder to the distance across the top of the cylinder is always the same. Write down what you think about this claim and how you could prove or disprove it.

Expose Beliefs

Share your views with others in your small groups. Select someone from your group to present the views of the group to the class.

Confront Beliefs

In your group, decide how you can test this claim. Get the necessary materials and test your ideas. Present your data in the form of a table. Prepare a graph based on your data table. Do you see a pattern? How does your data compare to your original thoughts about the cylinders?

Accommodate the Concept

Do your findings agree with the other groups' results? Write a statement representing the pattern you have detected. How can you express the relationship you found in your table, graph, or statement in the form of a mathematical equation? What can you conclude about the original claim?

Extend the Concept

In what real-life situations might this information be useful?

Go Beyond

What other questions or ideas would you like to explore about this concept?

APPENDIX II. CCM LESSON-PLANNING SUMMARY

Prepare before designing a conceptual change lesson.

♦ Explicitly identify the specific topic, concept(s), skills, processes, dispositions, and habits of mind that will be targeted by the lesson.

♦ Review what the relevant content standards have to say about appropriate expectations for students at the grade level.

♦ Explore what the teacher knows or may need to learn more about in regard to the chosen topic in order to teach the lesson effectively; for example, most topics have underlying concepts and connections that are essential for guiding students to understand at the desired level and avoid inadvertent development of misconceptions.

♦ Identify prerequisite understandings and skills—those things that students should already know and be able to do before this lesson.

♦ Identify the diversity of specific preconceptions and prior knowledge these students bring to the classroom in regard to the targeted topic, concepts, skills, and processes, using personalized and relevant pre-assessments such as interviews.

Use the information to develop the lesson.

♦ Develop lesson-specific expectations that take into account all of the above information, especially information revealed by student pre-assessments. Develop expectations for skills, processes, and dispositions, as well as content.

♦ Design an assessment plan to measure student progress toward each expectation. As noted in Chapter 9, it is important to assess learners on all expectations, but only certain expectations should be graded. Assessment should be aligned with both the expectations and the experiences students have in connection with the lesson.

♦ Develop the CCM lesson, including instructional strategies that will be used during each phase, materials students might need or request to conduct their explorations, and the number of class periods that might be involved. A list or table such as demonstrated below may be helpful. Additional columns can be added to meet the organizational style of individual teachers.

Phases of CCM lesson	Instructional strategies	Materials and resources	Class periods
Commit	[What is the challenge and how will students record their individual ideas?]		
Expose	[What and how will they share?]		
Confront	[What will they do to test their ideas and how will the teacher facilitate?]		
Accommodate	[What will students and teachers do as they work toward understanding?]		
Extend	[Students identify connections.]		
Go beyond	[Students provide new ideas, reach beyond familiar contexts.]		

Plan to evaluate lesson effectiveness.

◆ Make a plan to write observations (such as how students are working with the materials, what questions they are asking, evidence of active thinking and struggling to understand, misconceptions that are expressed, difficulties with skills and processes) and consider other data (such as assessments and student products) during and after the lesson.

◆ Reflect on these observations to decide:

• If it is necessary to loop back through all or part of another CCM sequence to reinforce or address remaining confusion or misunderstanding about the topic.

• What revisions to the lesson would improve it for the next time it is used.

• What were the most effective and least effective parts of the lesson in helping students to meet the expectations.

• What is needed to become more proficient in the design and implementation of CCM lessons.

APPENDIX III. ABOUT THE AUTHORS

Diane L. Schmidt

Diane Schmidt is the Director of the Whitaker Center for Science, Mathematics, and Technology Education and Assistant Professor in the College of Education at Florida Gulf Coast University. She received her BS in Special Education from Southern Illinois University, her MA in Instructional Design from Governor's State University, and her EdD in Curriculum and Instruction from the University of Central Florida.

Diane teaches a variety of courses at the undergraduate and graduate levels, including *Science Methods, Mathematics Content and Processes, Integrated Science and Mathematics, Trends in Mathematics Education*, and *Curriculum and Instruction*. Diane has over 20 years of teaching experience in K-12 public schools that includes both regular and special education classrooms at the elementary and middle school levels. She has directed and implemented professional development projects and conducted research in the areas of inquiry-based practices in science and mathematics, as well as other areas of the curriculum. Diane has served as Program Director for the Suncoast Area Center for Educational Enhancement, providing professional development in science and mathematics to classroom teachers throughout Florida.

Her current research and grant-funded projects reflect her commitment to fostering the use of inquiry-based practices. Diane is currently leading three Mathematics and Science Partnership projects in 30 Florida school districts. As lead curriculum developer for these projects, Diane has incorporated the use of the Conceptual Change Model for teaching of advanced science and mathematics content to teachers in grades 3-8. Her vision of all students actively and mentally engaged in meaningful learning provides direction for all her activities.

Barbara Woodworth Saigo

Barbara Saigo has had a varied career over nearly 40 years, with experience as a biology faculty member at the University of Wisconsin-Eau Claire and University of Northern Iowa; as a science education faculty member at St. Cloud State University (Minnesota); as assistant to a University President at UW-EC; and as Director of Sponsored Programs at Southeastern Louisiana University.

Barbara has directed grant projects for teacher professional development in science and mathematics and has consulted for universities, schools, and state education departments in science and environmental education. She has served on numerous national grant-proposal review panels, been active in professional societies, and presented nationally and internationally. Since 1979, she has coauthored university and high school texts and books for improving teaching and learning. She has been a publisher since 1993.

Barbara holds a BA in Biology from Willamette University, Salem, Oregon; MA in Zoology (emphasis in Natural History and Ecology) from Oregon State University, Corvallis; and PhD in Science Education from the University of Iowa. While completing her MA, she also completed all requirements for secondary teaching in biology. Her desire, throughout her career, has been to share and encourage curiosity, knowledge, and wonder about our fascinating natural world, among people of all ages. This she has done through formal and informal teaching, both face-to-face and through writing. Her hope is to encourage scientific literacy and caring stewardship based upon the development of deep understanding and appreciation of how the world works.

Joseph I. Stepans

Joe Stepans is Professor Emeritus of Science and Mathematics Education at the University of Wyoming. He received his BS in Physics from California State University, Stanislaus. His MS in Physics and PhD in Science Education are from the University of Wyoming. Joe has thirty years of teaching experience, including at the secondary level in Wyoming public schools and the university level at the University of Wyoming and Bu-Ali Sina University, Tehran, Iran.

Throughout his career, Joe has been guided by a concern for the value that students bring to the classroom and the respect with which their ideas are treated. He has investigated the nature and sources of students' misconceptions in science and mathematics and ways to help students overcome these. That work, reflected in some forty publications (books and articles) led to development of the research-based Conceptual Change Model that is the structural foundation of this book. He has presented at over 300 meetings of teachers and teacher education leaders across the United States and internationally, including Costa Rica, Iran, Panama, Malaysia, Puerto Rico, Spain, Chile, and the Republic of China.

Joe has provided service and leadership in the Association for Educators of Teachers of Science, International Consortium for Research in Science and Mathematics Education, National Science Teachers Association, Northern Rocky Mountain Educational Research Association, School Science and Mathematics Association, National Staff Development Council, and Wyoming Science Teachers Association. He has worked to implement sustainable professional development in several states, with collaborative support from grants and school districts. He is currently working on the application of the Conceptual Change Model to multiple subject areas beyond science and mathematics.

APPENDIX IV. ABOUT THE REVIEWERS

Robert E. Yager, Science Education Center, Professor of Science Education, The University of Iowa

Robert Yager was born and educated in Iowa. He earned a bachelor's degree in biology from the University of Northern Iowa and master's and doctoral degrees in plant physiology at the University of Iowa. Having started his career as a high school science teacher, he has been on the faculty at the University of Iowa since 1956, where he has directed 130 PhD dissertations. He has over 600 publications, including the recent *Exemplary Science Program* monographs for the National Science Teachers Association (NSTA). He was an active contributor to the *National Science Education Standards.* Dr. Yager has directed 150 national projects for science teachers. He has worked on several international projects (Japan, Korea, Taiwan, and Europe), often in association with former students. Dr. Yager has been president of seven national professional associations, including NSTA. He is widely known for his work in Science-Technology-Society education, which has been active in the U.S. since 1980.

James A. Shymansky, E. Desmond Lee Professor of Science Education, University of Missouri-St. Louis

Jim Shymansky was Professor of Science Education at the University of Iowa from 1973-1997. Jim has authored or coauthored more than 80 journal articles, 3 books, and 18 textbooks and workbooks. A few of his professional leadership activities include: President of the National Association for Research in Science Teaching (2005-2006); Senior Editor, International Journal of Science and Mathematics Education (2003-present); Past Editor, Journal of Research on Science Teaching (1980-84); Senior Editor, International Journal of Science and Mathematics Education. He holds a BS in Education from Bloomsburg State College, an MS in Physics from Indiana State University, and a PhD from Florida State University.

Linda Ray, Professor of Literacy and Associate Dean of Undergraduate Studies in the College of Education, Florida Gulf Coast University

Linda Ray received her bachelor's degree from the University of Dayton in elementary education, a master's degree in special education from the University of South Florida, and a doctorate in curriculum and instruction in special education and reading education from the University of South Florida. She teaches courses in literacy at both the graduate and undergraduate levels. Dr. Ray is a Faculty Fellow with the Family Literacy and Reading Education (FLaRE) grant project in Florida, an invited participant in the national Higher Education Collaborative project, and a grant reviewer for Reading First, Florida.

Diana Wiig, Department of Elementary and Early Childhood Education, University of Wyoming

For over twenty years, Diana Wiig was an elementary school educator. She served on numerous curriculum and professional development committees. In addition, she was the Science and Mathematics Coordinator for her school district. Presently, she is teaching methods courses in literacy and science and mathematics to pre-service teachers at the University of Wyoming. She designs and delivers professional development opportunities in mathematics and science in school districts around the state and is a facilitator for the WyTRIAD professional development program. In her spare time, she is the director and instructor of resident summer astronomy camps in Rock Springs, Wyoming. Diana received her BA in Elementary Education at the University of Northern Iowa, MA in Curriculum and Instruction, and PhD in Curriculum and Instruction at the University of Wyoming.

Timothy T. Couch, Jr., K-12 Professional Development Coordinator, The Whitaker Center for Science, Mathematics, and Technology Education, Florida Gulf Coast University

Tim serves as coordinator, mentor, and coach for teachers participating in a Mathematics and Science Partnership (MSP) project at Florida Gulf Coast University, funded by the Florida Department of Education. In this role, he serves on the curriculum development team for summer institutes, facilitates the pedagogical aspects of the institutes, develops and delivers follow-up workshops in the planning and implementation of CCM lessons, and provides one-on-one support to teachers in the project. Mr. Couch has taught 5th-8th grade science at a Title I school in Fort Myers, Florida, using the CCM with all levels of students (ESE, ESOL, regular, and gifted). Tim received his BS in Secondary Science Education from Florida Gulf Coast University and is currently finishing his Master's degree in Curriculum and Instruction at FGCU.

APPENDIX V. A PROFESSIONAL INVITATION

In response to teachers' suggestions, we are hoping to assemble and publish a set of brief but helpful case studies about implementation of specific CCM lessons. The details of publication are tentative—this may be an electronically distributed publication, for example, or it may be a book.

A modest honorarium will be offered for selected contributions, as well as identification of authorship. All materials submitted must meet editorial review criteria in order to be selected for publication. Some developmental assistance will be available to help put materials into final form.

We encourage you to contact us with preliminary drafts as well as full case studies.

We envision that case studies might include the following parts.

1. Pre-assessment interview questions and student responses
2. Your reactions to and reflection on student interviews
3. All elements of the lesson plan (as in Appendix I)
4. Your reflections on designing and implementing the lessons
5. Assessments you used and your thoughts about them
6. Your classroom observations and reflections about the lessons, how your students responded to them, and how your thoughts about teaching changed and developed
7. Any changes you might make as a result of the experience
8. Any involvement by colleagues in modeling, observing, coaching, or sharing views
9. Your conclusions and reflections about the experience, other comments you would like to make

If you are interested in contributing to such a project, contact Saiwood Publications with your ideas. We hope to include the experiences of teachers at all levels, including those who may be teaching, interning, or home-schooling, across the full K-12 spectrum (grade levels, special needs, gifted, English language learners, *etc.*).

We are interested in diverse curricular areas—mathematics, the sciences, social sciences, language arts, music and other arts, health and physical education, and foreign languages, for example.

Please send all communication in writing. Email Saiwood Publications at *saiwood@aol.com* or send a letter by First Class Mail. Our postal address is on the Copyright Page at the front of the book.

APPENDIX VI. READER FEEDBACK REQUEST

Thank you for using our book! We welcome your feedback to inform the next revision. Specifically, we would like to know:

♦ Things about the book that you liked and found helpful
♦ Constructive criticisms
♦ Suggestions for improvement
♦ Reflections about
    – The Conceptual Change Model
    – The book
    – The authors
    – How your students reacted
    – Your experiences
♦ How you learned about the book
♦ Other comments you would like to share

Please send all communication in writing, preferably as email to Saiwood Publications at *saiwood@aol.com*.

Thank you.